Sight Wor Extravaganza!

120 Sight Words that are Integral for Reading Success!

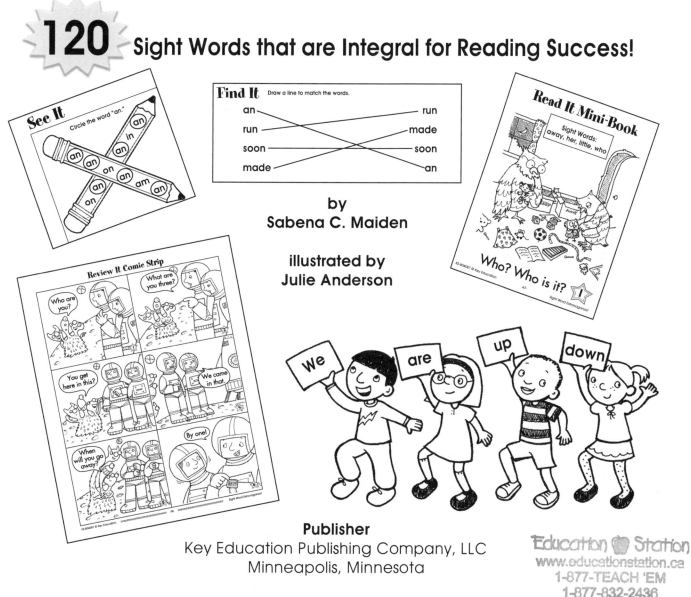

by
Sabena C. Maiden

illustrated by
Julie Anderson

Publisher
Key Education Publishing Company, LLC
Minneapolis, Minnesota

www.keyeducationpublishing.com

CONGRATULATIONS ON YOUR PURCHASE OF A KEY EDUCATION PRODUCT!

The editors at Key Education are former teachers who bring experience, enthusiasm, and quality to each and every product. Thousands of teachers have looked to the staff at Key Education for new and innovative resources to make their work more enjoyable and rewarding. We are committed to developing educational materials that will assist teachers in building a strong and developmentally appropriate curriculum for young children.

PLAN FOR GREAT TEACHING EXPERIENCES WHEN YOU USE
EDUCATIONAL MATERIALS FROM KEY EDUCATION PUBLISHING COMPANY, LLC

About the Author

Sabena Maiden is a former preschool and middle school teacher who taught for more than 10 years before making the move to publishing. She was hired by a leading educational publisher as a copywriter in advertising and later transferred to product development to work as a book editor. Since starting a family, she is now a freelance writer and editor. Having helped produce dozens of books, her work primarily includes educational, Christian, ESL, and literacy publications.

Dedication

To Mrs. Williams and Mrs. Wishon. Thank you for educating so many with love.
And always to my husband and children, my favorite reading group.

Credits

Author: Sabena C. Maiden
Publisher: Sherrill B. Flora
Illustrator: Julie Anderson
Editors: Karen Seberg and Claude Chalk
Cover Production: Annette Hollister-Papp
Page Layout: Key Education Staff
Cover Photographs: © Comstock, © ShutterStock,

Key Education welcomes manuscripts and product ideas from teachers.
For a copy of our submission guidelines, please visit our Web site or send a self-addressed, stamped envelope to:

Key Education Publishing Company, LLC
Acquisitions Department
7309 West 112th Street
Minneapolis, Minnesota 55438

Copyright Notice

Standard Book Number: 978-1-602680-75-3
Sight Word Extravaganza!
Copyright © 2011 by Key Education Publishing Company, LLC
Minneapolis, Minnesota 55438

Contents

Introduction

Sight Word Extravaganza! covers 120 sight words that are integral for students' reading success. The book is organized into 30 five-page sections; each section introduces four new words. The sections are arranged as follows:

See It and Find It: The first page of each section contains a See It individual lesson that briefly introduces each word with an activity, such as writing, tracing, connecting the dots, cutting and pasting, or coloring. These simple exercises are followed by a Find It activity to test student recognition of each word with matching or crossing out words that don't belong.

Try It Together: The second page is called Try It Together. This class activity involves a recognizable or predictable rebus story that includes the section's four new sight words. The stories are from popular children's songs, nursery rhymes, recognizable excerpts from favorite children's literature, and finally, original, but predictable, rhymes.

Do It and Play It: The third page starts with a Do It multisensory activity to practice using the new sight words through painting, singing, building, marching, or other engaging experiences. Then, there is a group or class activity called Play It where students use the words while participating in a physical and/or mental game.

Read It: The fourth page, Read It, is for students to read a fun, very short story in the form of a mini-book that contains all four new sight words. Illustrations provide context and interest for the student.

Review It Comic Strips: The fifth page ends the section with Review It Comic Strips. At the conclusion of each section (except for the first one), students will read a story that incorporates some of the words from the past sections. As students progress through the book and improve their skills, the Review It stories increase in difficulty.

Reproduciible Word Cards: Following the activity sections, the 120 sight words are provided on easy-to-use, reproducible word cards. Copy them on card stock or colored paper or enlarge them as needed for classroom activities and laminate them for durability. You may wish to create a complete set of cards for each student to practice with or to take home for further reinforcement.

It is recommended to go through this book in the order in which it is presented because the words and stories build upon one another. As students achieve success in the easier beginning activities and passages, they will strengthen their word recognition skills and increase reading confidence. And, as they notice that they actually know so many words by sight, they will be able to translate that knowledge into other classroom reading and beyond. Soon, students will realize that they are real readers!

See It

New Words: and, he, she, you

Trace the word "and."

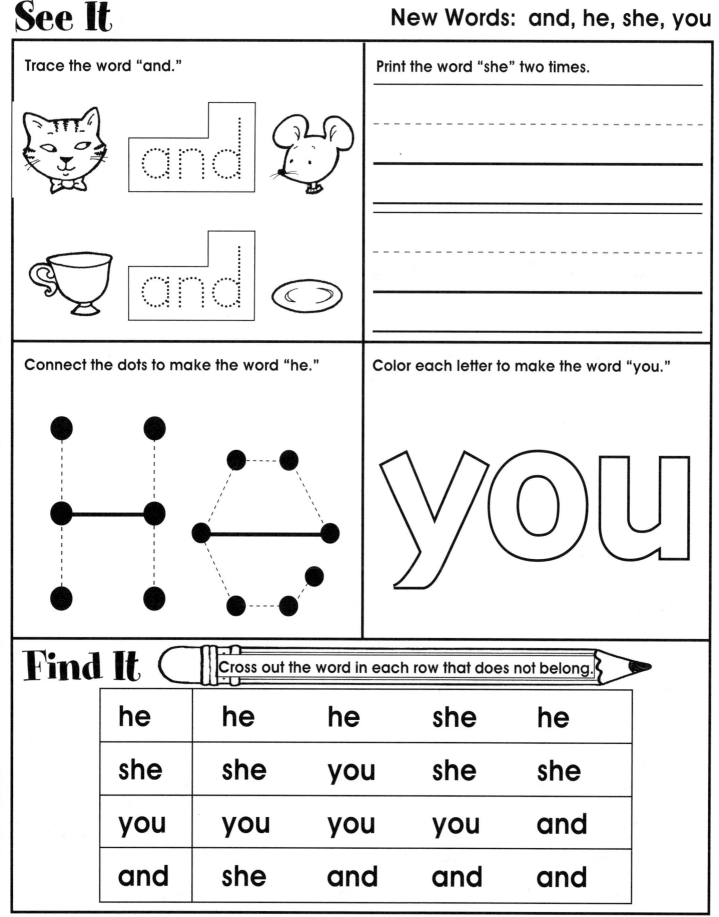

Print the word "she" two times.

Connect the dots to make the word "he."

Color each letter to make the word "you."

Find It

Cross out the word in each row that does not belong.

he	he	he	she	he
she	she	you	she	she
you	you	you	you	and
and	she	and	and	and

Name: _____

Directions: Cut out and paste the pictures to complete the story.

Pat-a-cake, pat-a-cake, [glue picture here] man,

Bake me a [glue picture here] as fast as **you** can.

Roll it **and** prick it **and** mark it with a "B"

And put it in the [glue picture here] for [glue picture here] **and** me!

Pat-a-cake, pat-a-cake, [glue picture here] man,

Bake me a [glue picture here] as fast as **you** can.

Roll it **and** prick it **and** mark it with a "B"

And put it in the [glue picture here]

for **she and he**!

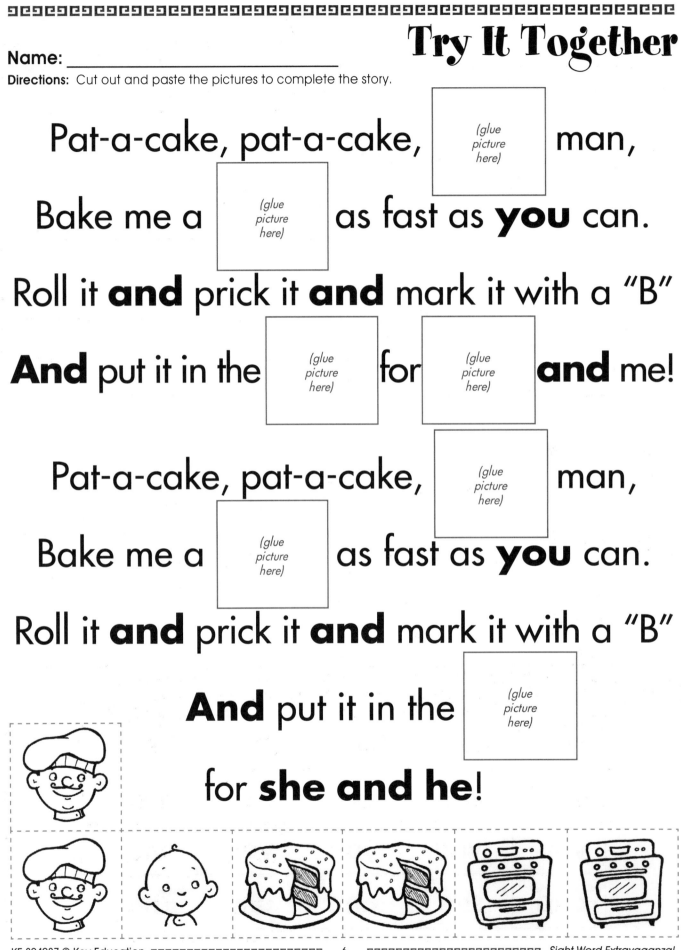

Do It

Bendable Letters and Words

Provide each student with three different-colored chenille craft sticks. Have students bend the chenille sticks to form each letter and make the new sight words. As students shape the words, give them the paper word cards (below) so that they can match up each letter correctly to check their work.

Play It

Answer Word Questions

Copy and cut out sets of new sight word cards (below), one set for each student. Have students sit in a circle around you. Instruct them to place all four word cards in their laps. Explain that you are going to give them hints about one of the words, and they will guess which word you chose. For example, say, "I am thinking of a word that rhymes with shoe," or "This word starts with /y/." Invite students to hold up the word card they think matches the clue. Provide up to three hints until most students are holding up the correct word. Increase the difficulty level of the clues to reinforce the words. Continue the activity until each sight word has been chosen at least twice and students demonstrate improved accuracy with their answers.

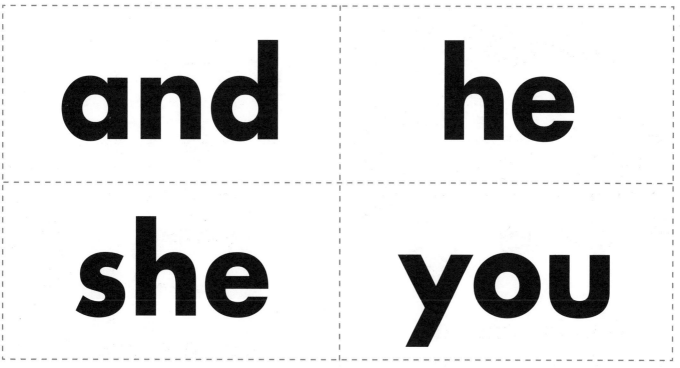

FOLD #1

You, he, and she!
We make three.

4

FOLD #2

Read It Mini-Book

Sight Words:
and, she, he, you

She and you.

1

See It

New Words: are, down, up, we

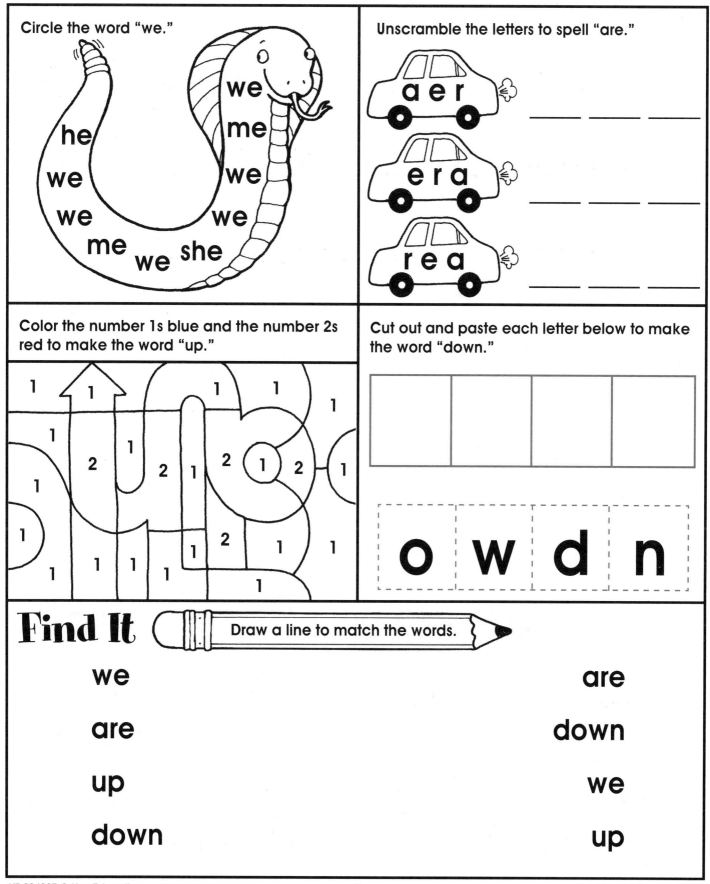

Circle the word "we."

Unscramble the letters to spell "are."

a e r _ _ _

e r a _ _ _

r e a _ _ _

Color the number 1s blue and the number 2s red to make the word "up."

Cut out and paste each letter below to make the word "down."

o w d n

Find It

Draw a line to match the words.

we   are

are   down

up   we

down   up

Directions: Cut out and paste the pictures to complete the story.

London (glue picture here) is falling **down**,

Falling **down**, falling **down**.

London (glue picture here) is falling **down**,

My fair (glue picture here) .

How **are we** going to (glue picture here) it **up**,

(glue picture here) it **up**, (glue picture here) it **up**?

How **are we** going to (glue picture here) it **up**,

My fair (glue picture here) ?

Do It

Sight Word March

Provide each student with a marker and an index card. Assign students one of the new sight words to write on their cards. Have students gather in four groups based on their words and line up in four single file lines. Once students are grouped and standing in their lines, explain that you will lead them in a chant from the front of the room. After students are familiar with the military-style cadence, lead them in a march around the room. Encourage each group to hold up their cards as their word is called out.

We are up.
We are down.
   (*students repeat*)
We are marching through the town.
   (*students repeat*)

We are up.
We are down. (*students repeat*)
We are singing all around.
   (*students repeat*)

We are up.
We are down. (*students repeat*)
We are ready to sit down. (*students repeat*)

Play It

Sight Word Concentration

Make sets of the new sight word cards, one set for each student (see pages 154–159). Divide the class into pairs and give two sets (eight cards) to each student pair. Instruct students to place all eight word cards facedown. Then, invite them to play a mini-game of Concentration. Explain that they will take turns turning over two cards to find word card matches. If a match is made, the student keeps the cards, and takes another turn. Have students play several rounds to reinforce their recognition of the sight words.

We are down.

We are up
and down.

FOLD #1

Read It Mini-Book

Sight Words:
are, down, up, we

4

We are clowns.

FOLD #2

We are up.

1

Review It Comic Strip

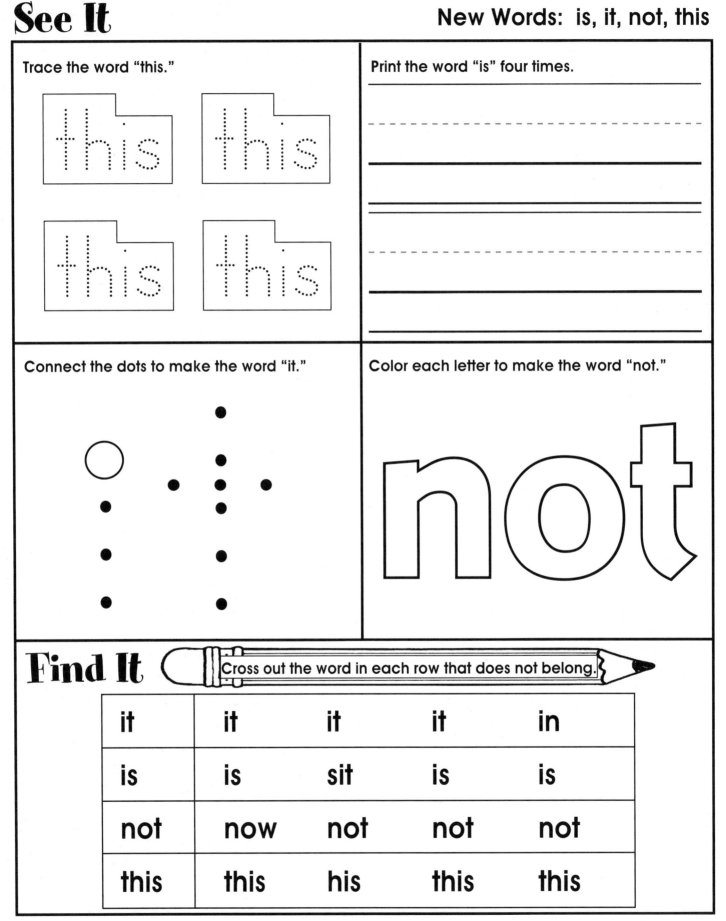

See It

Trace the word "this."

this this

this this

Print the word "is" four times.

Connect the dots to make the word "it."

Color each letter to make the word "not."

not

Find It

Cross out the word in each row that does not belong.

it	it	it	it	in
is	is	sit	is	is
not	now	not	not	not
this	this	his	this	this

Name: _____

Directions: Cut out and paste the pictures to complete the story.

This little *(glue picture here)* took a big leap,

This little *(glue picture here)* took a small leap,

This little *(glue picture here)* leaped sideways,

And **this** little *(glue picture here)* **not** at all.

And, **this** little *(glue picture here)* went

hippity, hippity, hippity hop,

And **it is** now all the way *(glue picture here)v* .

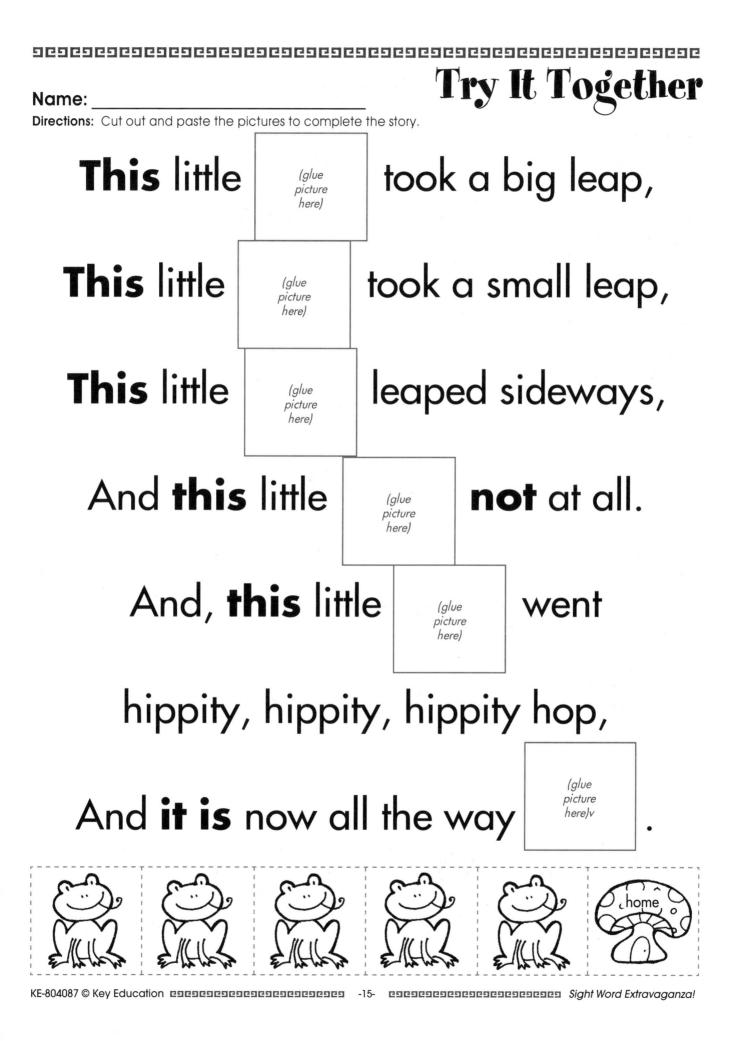

Do It

Roll-a-Word

Collect sets of dice. On each die face, tape one of the new sight words. For a pair of dice, you will use each word three times. Copy the Sight Words Tally Sheet (see example) on the board. Divide the class into pairs and instruct each pair to copy the Tally Sheet information on a piece of paper. Then, give each pair of students a set of sight words dice. As students take turns rolling the dice, they will mark their tally sheets to record the sight words rolled.

SIGHT WORDS TALLY SHEET	
it	ＨＨ
is	ＩＩ
not	ＩＩＩＩ
this	ＨＨ ＩＩＩ

Play It

Word Bowling

Set up three to five bowling lanes in your classroom with eight toy bowling pins (or use clean plastic soda bottles) for each lane. Label each pin with a new sight word, two pins for each word. Assign groups of students to the lanes. Have students take turns rolling a playground ball to knock down as many pins as possible. Then, the student retrieves and resets those pins, announcing each pin's sight word as it is replaced.

This is not it.

FOLD #1

Is this it?

This is it!

Read It Mini-Book

Sight Words:
is, it, not, this

Is this it?

FOLD #2

Sight Word Extravaganza!

Review It Comic Strip

Circle the word "my."

Unscramble the letters to spell "three."

Color the number 1s blue and the number 2s red to make the word "with."

Cut out and paste each letter below to make the word "play."

l p y a

Find It

Draw a line to match the words.

with	three
my	play
three	with
play	my

Name: _____

Directions: Cut out and paste the pictures to complete the story.

Oh, playmate,

Come out and **play with** me.

And, bring your (glue picture here) **three**.

Climb up **my** (glue picture here) (glue picture here) .

Slide down **my** (glue picture here)

Into my cellar (glue picture here) .

And, we'll be jolly (glue picture here) , forevermore.

dollies

friends

Do It

Blindfolded Reading

Form the letters for each new sight word from clay or modeling dough. Allow the clay letters for each word to harden into one solid shape so that there are four distinct word shapes. Invite students to put on a blindfold and try to determine by touch which new sight word each shape represents. After all students have had a turn, provide modeling dough for them to practice forming their own sight word shapes. Encourage students to use a different color for each letter in the words, which will make the individual letters stand out and emphasize correct spelling.

Play It

Beanbag Word Toss

Use tape and markers to label four beanbags, each with a new sight word. Label four containers with the matching sight words and place them near the board. Have students line up about 10' (3 m) away from the containers. Allow them to take turns tossing each word beanbag into the corresponding container. Then, write just one of the sight words on the board at a time so that students can practice that target word. Continue play until each student has had at least one opportunity to review all four sight words.

3 Pets play with pets.

FOLD #1

2 The three pets play.

---

4 My three pets sleep.

FOLD #2

Read It Mini-Book

Sight Words:
my, play, three, with

1 My pets play.

Review It Comic Strip

Trace the word "in."

Print the word "I" six times.

Connect the letters to make the word "so."

Color each letter to make the word "like."

Find It

Cross out the word in each row that does not belong.

in	is	in	in	in
I	I	I	L	I
like	like	like	look	like
so	so	is	so	so

Name: _____

Directions: Cut out and paste the pictures to complete the story.

Twinkle, twinkle, little [glue picture here] ,

How **I** wonder what you are.

Up above the [glue picture here] **so** high,

Like a [glue picture here] **in** the sky.

Twinkle, twinkle, little [glue picture here] ,

How **I** wonder what you are.

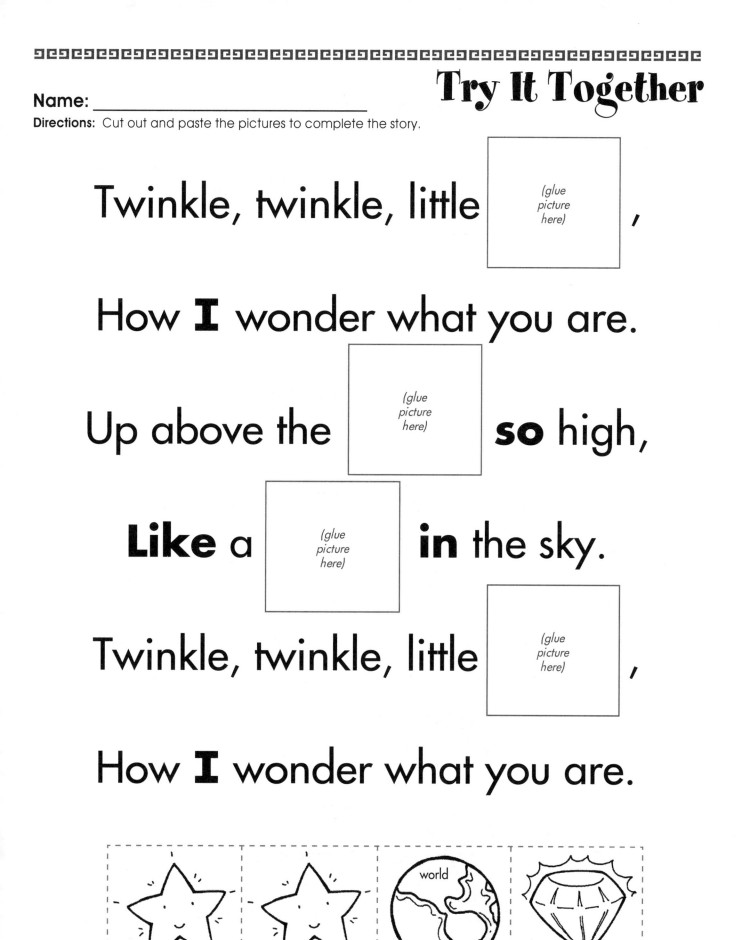

Do It

Stick-On Sight Words

Provide each student with a different popular children's book and a small set of mini self-stick notes. Allow students to work in pairs. Instruct them to find the new sight words *I*, *in*, *like*, and *so* in their books. When they find one of the new words, one student should write it on a self-stick note and place the note over the word in the book. The student's partner can help if a word is misspelled. Then, have students switch roles for the second book.

Play It

Word Hop

Use tape on the floor to make a grid with three rows and four columns. Randomly place a new sight word in each section of the grid by writing the word on a piece of tape or using a word card (see pages 154–159). Each new sight word will be used three times. Finally, make a large word card for each sight word. Invite two students to approach the grid. Hold up a large word card and name the word. Then, let the rest of the class cheer the students on as the duo hops to the words on the grid. The object is to have each student hop to the various sight words with accuracy. Play until each student has hopped through the sight word grid at least once.

I like it in this.

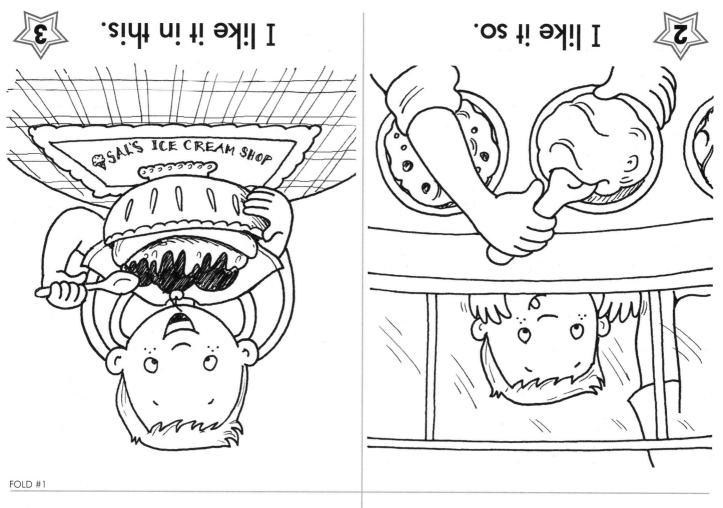

SAL'S ICE CREAM SHOP

FOLD #1

2

I like it so.

I so like it.

Read It Mini-Book

Sight Words:
I, in, like, so

Sal's

ICE CREAM

I like it.

FOLD #2

KE-804087 © Key Education   -27-   *Sight Word Extravaganza!*

Review It Comic Strip

See It

New Words: by, me, one, to

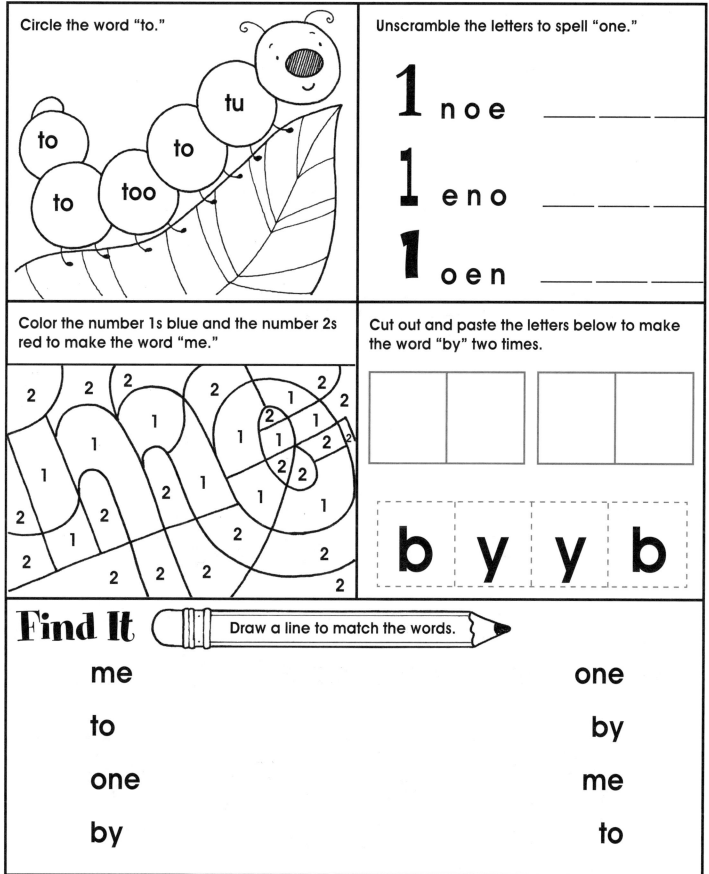

Circle the word "to."

Unscramble the letters to spell "one."

1 n o e _____

1 e n o _____

1 o e n _____

Color the number 1s blue and the number 2s red to make the word "me."

Cut out and paste the letters below to make the word "by" two times.

b   y   y   b

Find It

Draw a line to match the words.

me

to

one

by

one

by

me

to

Name: _____

Directions: Cut out and paste the pictures to complete the story.

Eeny, meeny, miny, moe,

Catch a [(glue picture here)] **by** the [(glue picture here)] .

If he hollers, let him [(glue picture here)] ,

Eeny, meeny, miny, moe.

My [(glue picture here)] told **me**

To pick the very best **one**–and you are it.

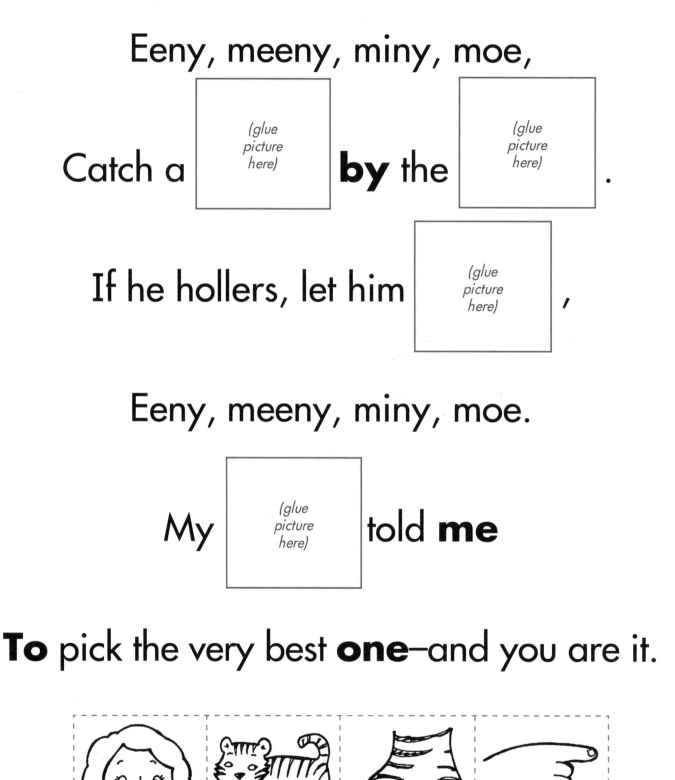

mother

toe

go

Do It

Writing in the Sand

For this group activity, fill one large, shallow container, such as a plastic swimming pool, with sand. If you wish students to work individually or in pairs, use several small containers, such as metal baking pans, dishpans, or plastic storage boxes. Add a little water to each container to dampen the sand until drawing with a finger leaves an impression. Display the new sight words for all students to see. Have them practice "writing" the words in the wet sand using their pointer fingers. To reward them for their work, provide students with sand and water toys and time to play and build.

Play It

Make-a-Move Sight Words

Use the tune and motions to the classic children's song "Head, Shoulders, Knees, and Toes" to reinforce the new sight words. Have students sing the sight word and touch each body part as follows: *to*—head, *me*—shoulders, *one*—knees, and *by*—toes. Then, give four student volunteers large sight word cards and ask them to stand at the front of the room, holding up the correct word as each sight word is sung. For extra fun, start off slowly and gradually increase the tempo. Choose four new students and sing the song again.

To, me, one, and by, one and by,
To, me, one, and by, one and by,
To, me, one, and by,
To, me, one, and by, one and by!

★ 3

To me?

FOLD #1

★ 2

One by me.

★ 4

To me.

FOLD #2

Read It Mini-Book

Sight Words:
by, me, one, to

One by one.

★ 1

Review It Comic Strip

See It

Trace the word "the."

Print the word "all" four times.

Connect the letters to make the word "when."

Color each letter to make the word "will."

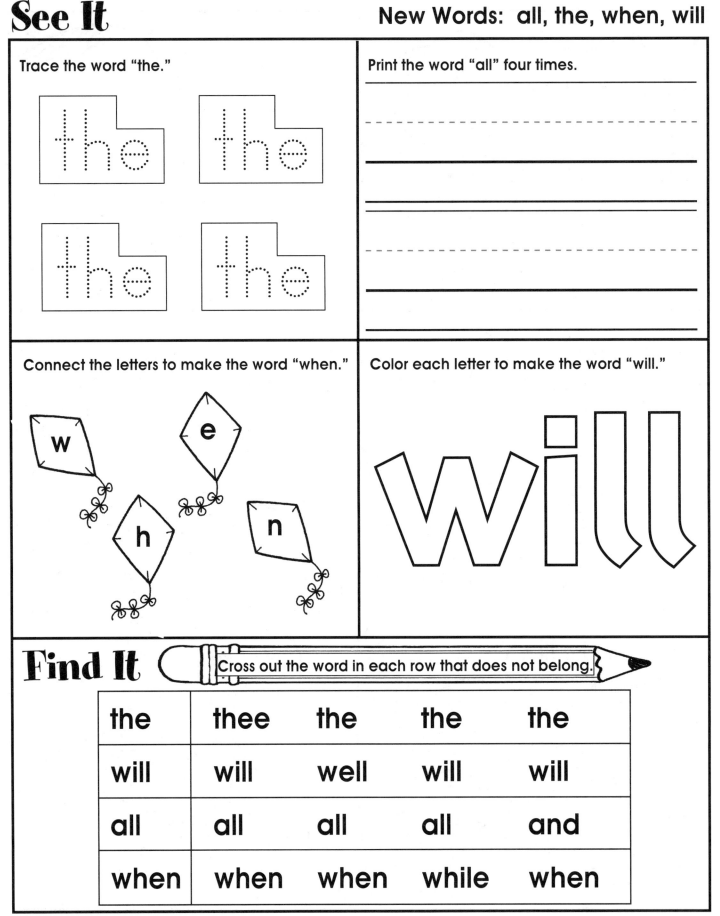

Find It

Cross out the word in each row that does not belong.

the	thee	the	the	the
will	will	well	will	will
all	all	all	all	and
when	when	when	while	when

Name: _____

Directions: Cut out and paste the pictures to complete the story.

Rock-a-bye _(glue picture here)_ in **the** _(glue picture here)_ top.

When the _(glue picture here)_ blows,

the _(glue picture here)_ **will** rock.

When the bough breaks,

the _(glue picture here)_ **will** fall,

And down **will** come _(glue picture here)_ ,

(glue picture here) , and **all**.

cradle

cradle   cradle

wind

• • • • • • • • • • • • Do It • • • • • • • • • • • •

Letter Blocks

Provide each student with a set of wooden letter blocks. Be sure that each set contains all of the letters needed to make the new sight words: *t, h, e, w, i, l, l, a, n.* (If enough blocks are not available, set up the activity in a center.) Provide minute timers; students should try to organize the letters for each sight word in less than one minute. Encourage them to build each word from top to bottom or left to right. After students have worked with the wooden blocks, provide each student with nine copies of the cube pattern (right) to make their own letter blocks. Have students write one letter per cube, repeating the letter on each face; then, cut out the pattern, fold, and tape or glue the flaps. Students can practice making sight words at their seats when they finish an activity early. Allow students to take their letter blocks home for further reinforcement.

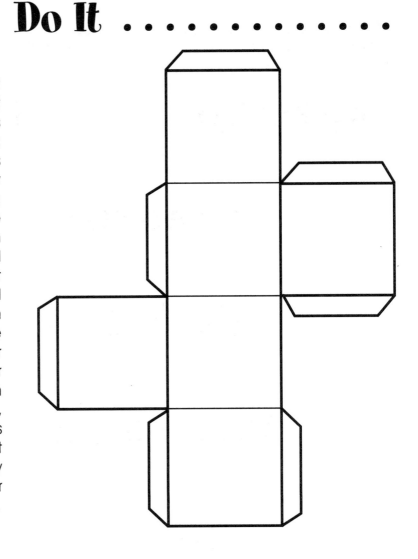

• • • • • • • • • • • • Play It • • • • • • • • • • • •

Word Cheers

Have a class pep rally and get students excited about learning their new sight words. If needed, show the class a video clip of a school pep rally or ballgame where cheering fans are yelling out their team name or colors. Divide the class into four groups and assign each group a new sight word: *all, the, when,* or *will.* Provide poster board and markers to the groups. Have each student make a sign highlighting the group's word. Then, have the groups gather together in four different areas of the room (or better yet, go outside). Allow each group a turn to cheer for their word and hold up their word signs to show their sight word spirit. Lead each group in a "Give me an *X*" cheer to spell out their word for the class to see and hear. After the sight word rally, display the signs around the room as daily reminders that learning new words can be fun.

Sight Words:
all, the, when, will

⑶ When will we all?

⑵ He will.

Read It Mini-Book

Sight Words:
all, the, when, will

⑷ The end.

FOLD #2

She will. ①

FOLD #1

Review It Comic Strip

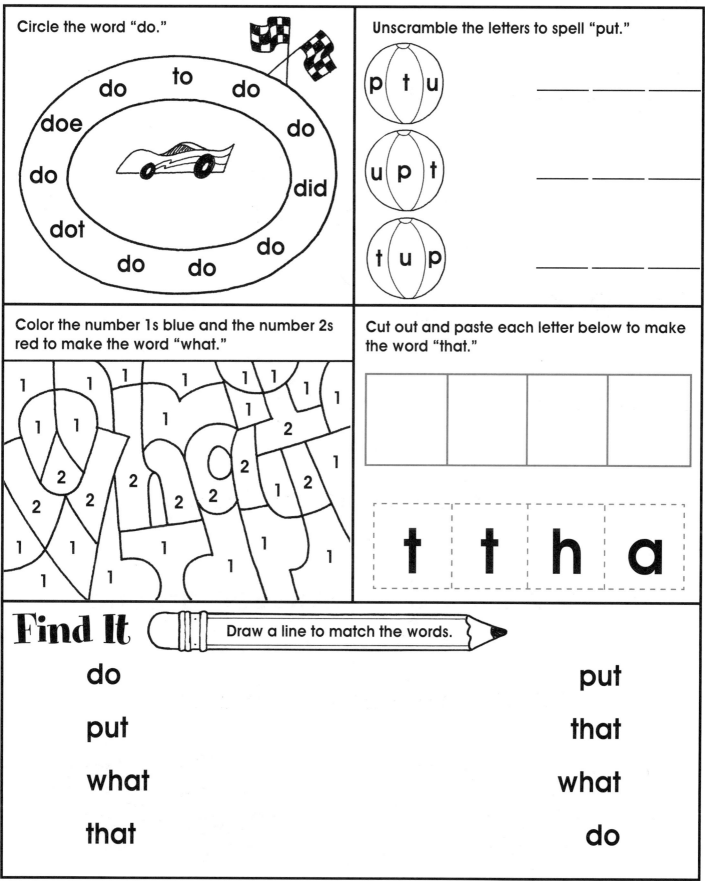

Circle the word "do."

do   to   do
doe
do   did
dot
do   do   do

Unscramble the letters to spell "put."

p t u   _____
u p t   _____
t u p   _____

Color the number 1s blue and the number 2s red to make the word "what."

Cut out and paste each letter below to make the word "that."

t   t   h   a

Find It

Draw a line to match the words.

do   put

put   that

what   what

that   do

Name: _____

Directions: Cut out and paste the pictures to complete the story.

You **put** your right [glue picture here] in,

You **put** your right [glue picture here] out;

You **put** your right [glue picture here] in,

And you [glue picture here] it all about.

You **do** the Hokey-Pokey,

And you [glue picture here] yourself around.

That's **what** it's all about!

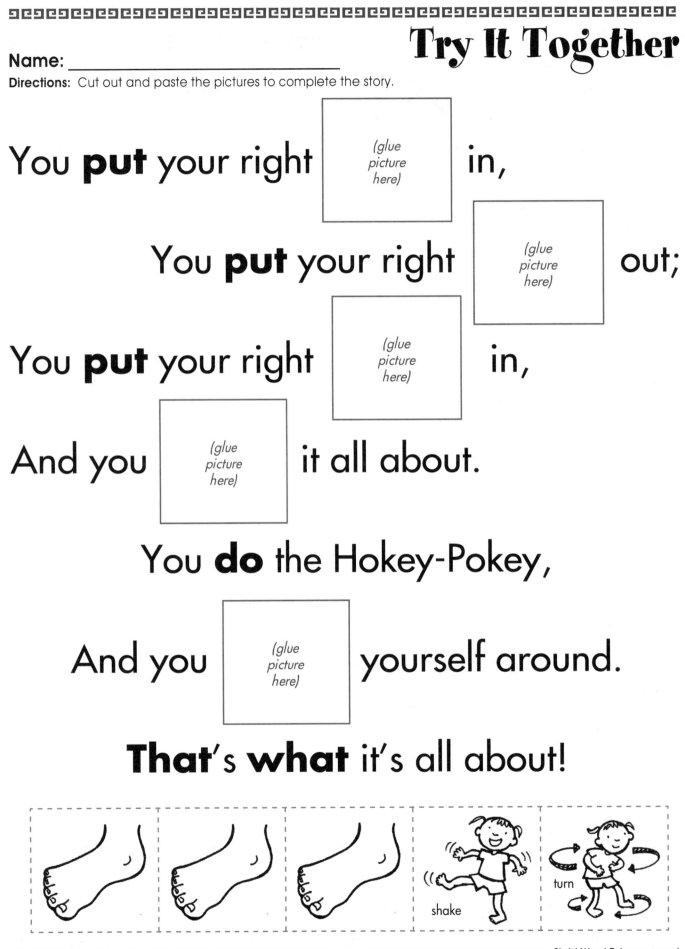

shake   turn

Do It

Smelly Words

Have students practice the new sight words by painting the words with inexpensive, kid-friendly "smelly paints." In small paper cups, mix the contents of one package of powdered, fruit-flavored drink mix and two tablespoons of warm water for each color of "paint." Provide four different "flavors" of paint so that students may use a different color for each letter in a word. Students may use paintbrushes or try cotton swabs for better writing control. Display the students' writing around the room. Then, as a class, admire their work by sitting back and enjoying a fruit juice drink or a snack of fresh fruit.

Play It

Word Search

Secretly assign each student one of the four sight words. Instruct students to walk round the room to find other classmates who share the same sight word with them, but without actually saying the word. For example, a student might say, "My word rhymes with *moo*." After all of the students with matching sight words find each other, reassign a new word to each student until every student has practiced all four words.

☆3☆ What do you do
with that?

☆2☆ What is what?

☆4☆ Put it in the trash!

FOLD #1

FOLD #2

Read It Mini-Book

Sight Words:
do, put, that, what

What is that?   ☆1☆

Review It Comic Strip

Trace the word "away."

away away

away away

Print the word "who" two times.

Connect the letters to make the word "little."

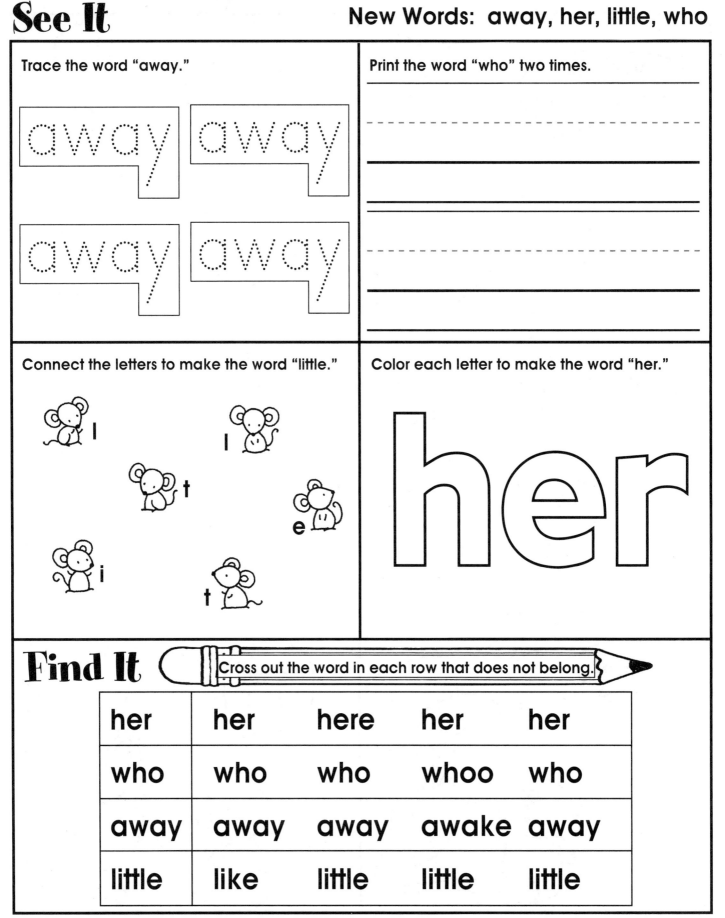

l

l

t

e

i

t

Color each letter to make the word "her."

her

Find It

Cross out the word in each row that does not belong.

her	her	here	her	her
who	who	who	whoo	who
away	away	away	awake	away
little	like	little	little	little

Name: _____

Directions: Cut out and paste the pictures to complete the story.

Little (glue picture here) sat on a (glue picture here) ,

Eating **her** curds and (glue picture here) ;

Along came a (glue picture here)

Who sat (glue picture here) beside **her**

And frightened (glue picture here) **away**.

Miss Muffet

Miss Muffet

tuffet

whey

down

• • • • • • • • • • • Do It • • • • • • • • • • •

Gobble Up Sight Words

Provide each student with four 3-inch (7.62 cm) in diameter balls of new, nontoxic modeling dough. After washing their hands, have them flatten each ball of dough and then use their fingers to make the impression of the letters of a new sight word. (Allow students to press small, plastic letters in the dough to make the words if needed.) Let the dough word molds dry completely. Then, lightly apply cooking spray to each of the molds and pour the students' favorite kind of juice into the molds. Place the filled molds in a freezer, allowing the ice word shapes to freeze solid. Have students gently remove the colorful and tasty ice words from the molds and enjoy "gobbling up" their sight words.

• • • • • • • • • • • Play It • • • • • • • • • • •

Word Hunt

Use index cards to create a set of the four new sight words for each student (or see pages 154–159). Then, hide the word cards around the room, making sure at least part of each card can be seen. Place some cards in obvious places, such as on a bulletin board or bookshelf. Announce that students are going on a word hunt. Explain that each student should find four different words. Other rules include: use only walking feet, no talking, and only keep four cards (but students can help their classmates). Tell students they will have about five minutes to complete their word hunt. When the time is up, see how many students found all four words. Finally, let students go on a word sort. Write or post the four sight words around the room. Explain the new rules: use only walking feet, no talking, and word cards must be correctly sorted and stacked neatly beneath the matching posted words.

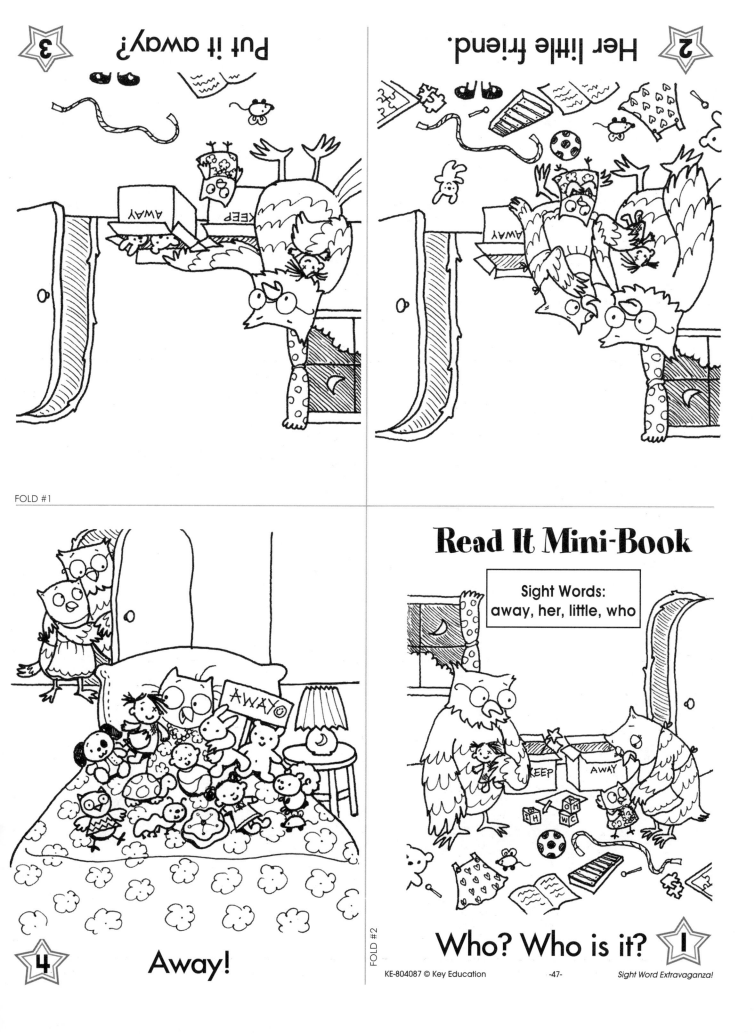

3 Put it away?

2 Her little friend.

FOLD #1

Read It Mini-Book

Sight Words:
away, her, little, who

4 Away!

FOLD #2

Who? Who is it? **1**

Review It Comic Strip

See It

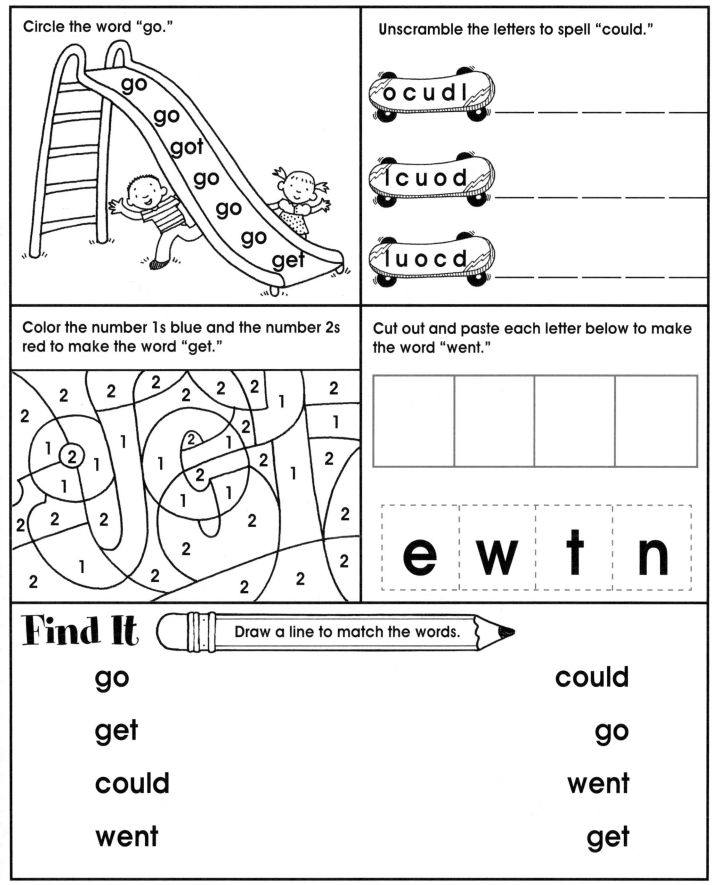

Circle the word "go."

Unscramble the letters to spell "could."

o c u d l _ _ _ _ _

l c u o d _ _ _ _ _

l u o c d _ _ _ _ _

Color the number 1s blue and the number 2s red to make the word "get."

Cut out and paste each letter below to make the word "went."

e   w   t   n

Find It

Draw a line to match the words.

go   could

get   go

could   went

went   get

Name: _____

Directions: Cut out and paste the pictures to complete the story.

It's raining, it's pouring;

The old [glue picture here] is snoring.

He bumped his [glue picture here] and **went** to [glue picture here]

And **could**n't **get** up in the morning.

[glue picture here] , [glue picture here] , **go** away;

Come again another day;

Little [glue picture here] wants to play.

Johnny   man   Rain   Rain   head

· · · · · · · · · · · · Do It · · · · · · · · · · · · · ·

Mosaic Words

Provide each student with several half sheets of colorful construction paper. Instruct students to cut the paper into small pieces of various regular and irregular shapes, approximately 1" (2.54 cm) square or smaller. Then, have students sort their paper shapes by color into piles. Give students white drawing paper, pencils, and gluesticks. Assign each student one (or more) new sight words. Using large letters, students should write one sight word on each piece of white paper. Finally, let students glue the small, colorful paper shapes on their printed letters to make mosaic-style sight word art. Display the finished mosaics around the classroom.

· · · · · · · · · · · · Play It · · · · · · · · · · · · · ·

Words That Are Verbs

Explain to students that all four new sight words are verbs; verbs are special words that may show activity. On the board, write the sight words and sentences shown below. Then, discuss how each verb, when used in the same sentence, makes something different happen.

Provide each student with a piece of drawing paper and colorful pencils or crayons. Have students fold their papers in half, both vertically and horizontally to make four sections. After rereading the sample sentences, they should copy one sentence in each section. Then, students may draw the sentences and compare the pictures to see the difference the verb makes.

③ Could I get it?

② She went and got it.

FOLD #1

④ We get it!

FOLD #2

Read It Mini-Book

Sight Words:
could, get, go, went

① I go to get it.

Review It Comic Strip

See It

Trace the word "but."

but but
but but

Print the word "was" two times.

Connect the letters to make the word "came."

c
m
a
e

Color each letter to make the word "had."

had

Find It

Cross out the word in each row that does not belong.

but	but	put	but	but
was	we	was	was	was
came	came	came	came	come
had	had	have	had	had

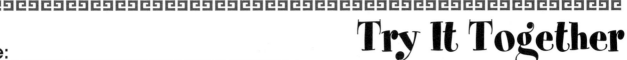

Name: _____

Try It Together

Directions: Cut out and paste the pictures to complete the story.

Old [glue picture here]

Went to the [glue picture here]

To fetch her poor [glue picture here] a [glue picture here] ;

But when she **came** there

The [glue picture here] **was** bare,

And so the poor [glue picture here] **had** none.

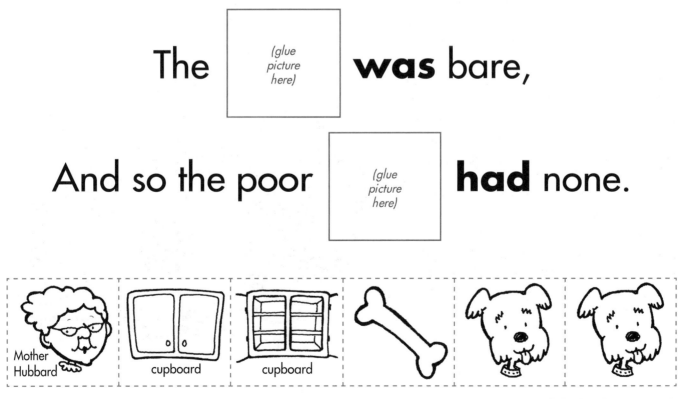

Mother Hubbard   cupboard   cupboard

Do It

Textile Words

Collect four different materials, such as fine sandpaper; bubble wrap; silk, rayon or other smooth, scrap fabric; and card stock. Cut out the letters for the new sight words using a different material for each word. Place all of the letters in a large paper bag. Invite students to take turns trying to spell out the words without looking at them. Have them close their eyes (or use a blindfold), reach into the bag, retrieve each letter, and use only a sense of touch to make the words. When the task is completed, have the students look at the letters to check each word.

Play It

Sight Word Duck, Duck, Goose

Have students sit in a circle and play a round of Duck, Duck, Goose. Then, explain that they will continue to play the fun chasing game, but, for the rest of the rounds, they will play while practicing the new sight words. Write the words on the board or display them on poster board or word cards. Before each new round, designate the "walking" word (for example, *came* for *duck*) and the "chasing" word (for example, *was* for *goose*). The walking player might say, "came, came, came, came, came, was!" Students love playing this game and the added benefit will be saying and hearing the new words.

He was home!

He came home.

2

FOLD #1

Read It Mini-Book

Sight Words:
but, came, had, was

SURPRISE!

4 But, he had had it.

FOLD #2

He had had it.

1

Review It Comic Strip

See It

Circle the word "yes."

Unscramble the letters to spell "boy."

oyb   byo   oby

___ ___ ___   ___ ___ ___

Connect the letters to make the word "for."

f

o

r

Cut out and paste each letter below to make the word "have."

e   h   a   v

Find It

Draw a line to match the words.

yes   for

have   boy

for   yes

boy   have

Name: _____

Directions: Cut out and paste the pictures to complete the story.

Baa, baa, black _[glue picture here]_ ,

Have you any _[glue picture here]_ ?

Yes sir, **yes** sir, _[glue picture here]_ _[glue picture here]_ full;

One **for** the _[glue picture here]_ ,

And one **for** the _[glue picture here]_ ,

And one **for** the little **boy**

Who lives _[glue picture here]_ the lane.

wool

3

master

dame

down

Do It

Felt Board Words

Using colorful scraps of felt, cut out the letters found in the new sight words: *a, b, e, f, h, o, r, s, v, y*. Stand a felt board (or make one by covering a large rectangle of cardboard or plywood with felt) on a table. Place the felt letters beside the board. Allow students to work in pairs to make each new sight word on the board. After students have succeeded in spelling each word, challenge them to use the same letters to make some of the other sight words they have been practicing. For example, they will be able to spell *are, by, he, her, she,* and *so.* You may wish to cut out more letters for additional sight words. If needed, post all of the previously learned sight words that can be made with the provided felt letters to ensure students' success and build confidence.

Sight Words Previously Learned:			
all	get	me	to
and	go	my	up
are	had	not	was
away	have	one	we
boy	he	play	went
but	her	put	what
by	I	she	when
came	in	so	who
could	is	that	will
do	it	the	with
down	like	this	yes
for	little	three	you

Play It

Team Word Toss

Create a fun and educational game to practice the new sight words using a rectangular piece of sturdy cardboard at least 5' (1.5 m) long and 2' (0.61 m) wide. Starting 6" (15.24 cm) from the top of the board, cut four 6" (15.24 cm) in diameter circular holes down the center. Leave at least 4" (10.16 cm) between the holes. Above each hole, use a thick marker to write one of the new sight words.

Place the board on the ground and angle it so that the top is at least 8" (20.32 cm) off the ground by taping two objects, such as paint bottles, to the back of the board. Divide the class into teams or play with a small groups. Allow students to take turns trying to toss four beanbags into the holes to earn points for their team. Have the top word worth four points, the second worth three points, the third worth two points, and the bottom word worth one point. Students may use tally marks to keep score. Periodically change the words' point values so that students aim for and focus on different sight words.

For me?

Yes, for the boy.

2

FOLD #1

Read It Mini-Book

Sight Words:
boy, for, have, yes

Yes, I have one
for him.

4

FOLD #2

KE-804087 © Key Education

-62-

Sight Word Extravaganza!

For the boy?

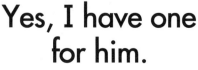

1

Review It Comic Strip

See It

Trace the word "know."

know know

know know

Print the word "find" two times.

Connect the letters to make the word "them."

Color each letter to make the word "has."

has

Find It

Cross out the word in each row that does not belong.

find	find	find	fond	find
them	them	them	then	them
has	has	has	has	had
know	know	knew	know	know

Name: _____

Directions: Cut out and paste the pictures to complete the story.

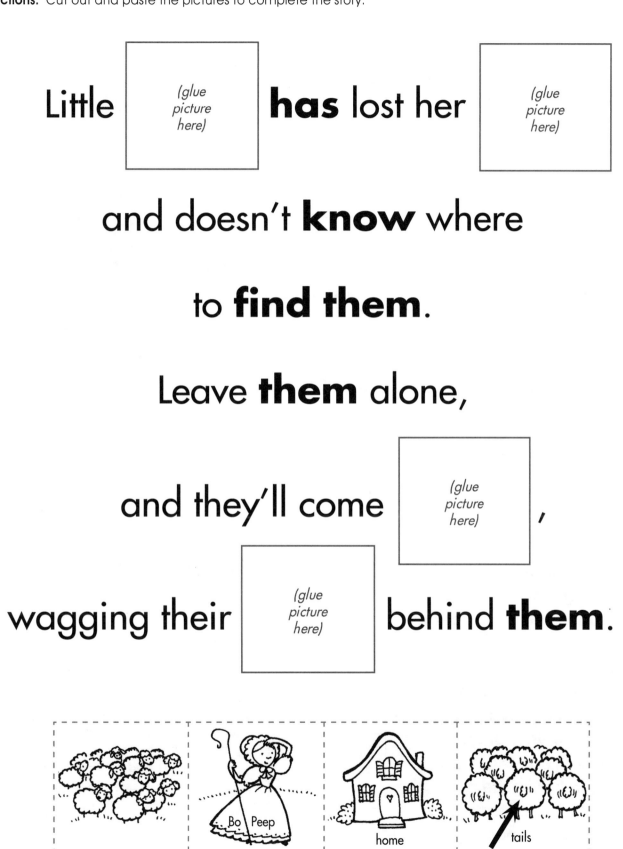

Little [(glue picture here)] **has** lost her [(glue picture here)]

and doesn't **know** where

to **find them**.

Leave **them** alone,

and they'll come [(glue picture here)] ,

wagging their [(glue picture here)] behind **them**.

Bo Peep

home

tails

Do It

The Coconut Shell Word Game

Divide the class into pairs. Provide each pair with eight self-stick notes, four in one color and four in another color. Instruct them to choose one of the colors of notes and write a new sight word on each note. Then, have them cover each of the words with the second color of self-stick notes so that the words are hidden. Now, students can play the Coconut Shell Game. The first student names one of the sight words. The student's partner mixes up the paired notes and lines them up in front of the student. The student then tries to find the named sight word by lifting a top self-stick note to read aloud the word written on the note underneath. When the word is discovered, have student pairs trade roles so that they each practice finding, recognizing, and reading the sight words several times.

Play It

Hopscotch Words

Create a hopscotch grid using masking tape to play inside or sidewalk chalk to play outside if the weather allows. Draw a classic hopscotch pattern or make up your own, writing the new sight words in place of numbers for students to hop on and over. To add extra fun as you reinforce the new words, insert the words into a classic playground jumping song for students to recite as each player hops on the grid. For example:

Teddy bear, teddy bear,
<u>find</u> the ground,
Teddy bear, teddy bear,
Turn around,
Teddy bear, teddy bear,
Walk <u>them</u> upstairs,
Teddy bear, teddy bear,
<u>know</u> your prayers,
Teddy bear, teddy bear,
Turn down the light,
Teddy bear, teddy bear,
<u>has</u> said good night!

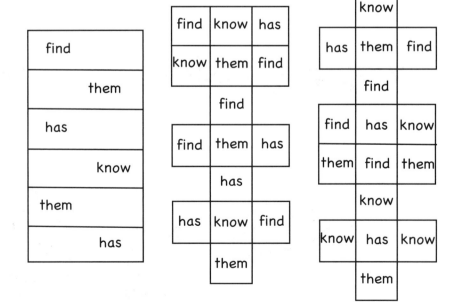

3 Find them!

FOLD #1

2 I do not know.

4 I know!

FOLD #2

Read It Mini-Book

Sight Words:
find, has, know, them

1 Who has them?

Review It Comic Strip

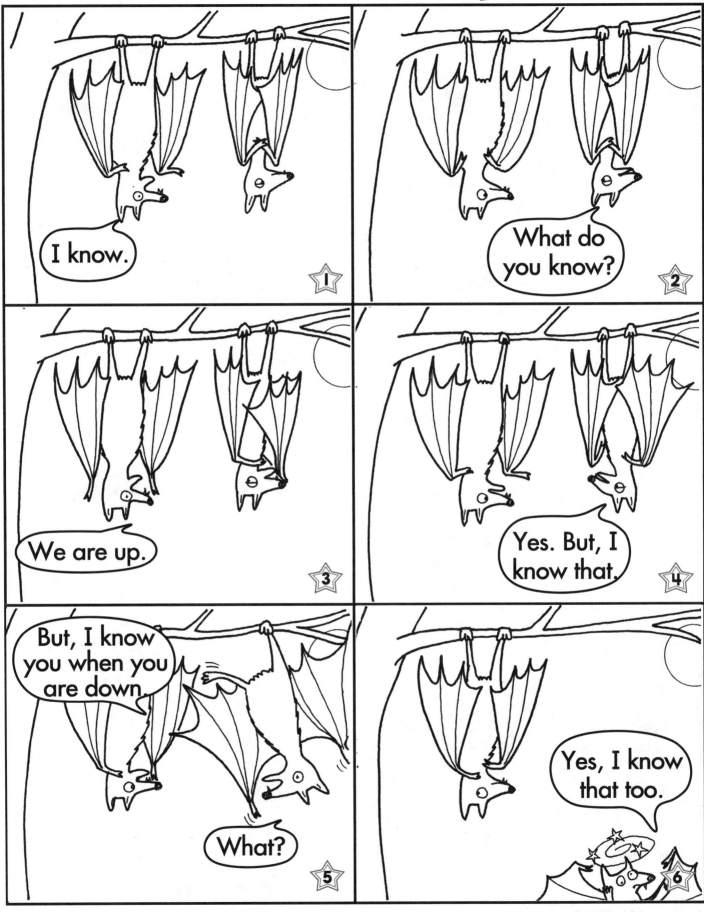

Circle the word "blue."

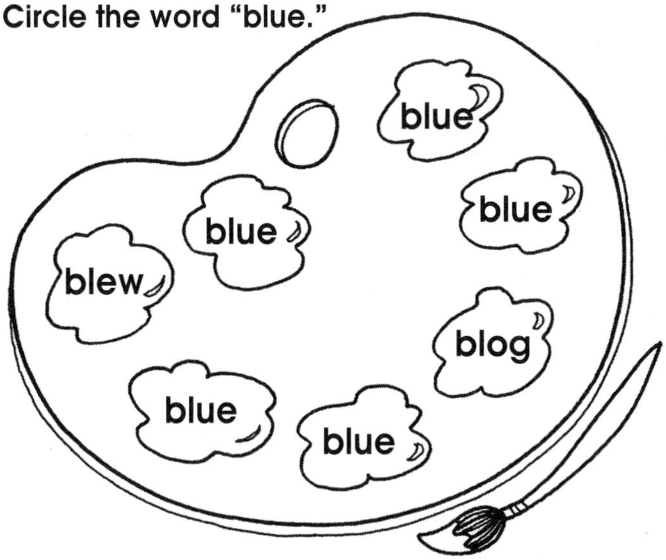

Unscramble the letters to spell "where."

wrehe

_____

eerwh

_____

rwehe

_____

Color the number 1s blue and the number 2s red to make the word "under."

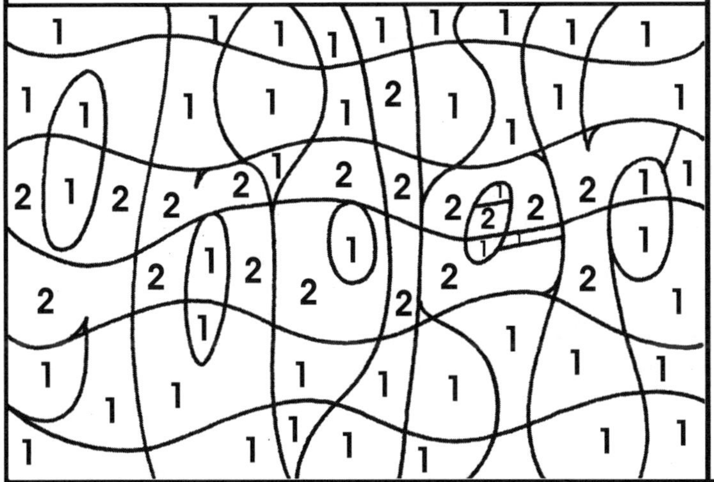

Cut out and paste each letter below to make the word "come."

o m c e

Find It

Draw a line to match the words.

blue   where

come   blue

under   come

where   under

Name: _____

Directions: Cut out and paste the pictures to complete the story.

Little [(glue picture here)] **Blue, come** blow your [(glue picture here)] .

The [(glue picture here)] are in the meadow;

the [(glue picture here)] are in the [(glue picture here)] .

Where is the [(glue picture here)]

who looks after the [(glue picture here)] ?

He's **under** a haystack, fast [(glue picture here)] .

Will you wake him? No, not I;

If I do, he's sure to cry.

Boy

Boy

Do It

Spell with Magnetic Letters

Provide each student with a set of plastic magnetic letters. Be sure that each set contains all of the letters needed to make the new sight words: *b, c, d, e, e, h, l, m, n, o, r, u, w.* (If there aren't enough magnetic letters available, set up the activity in a center.) Also, provide a magnetic board or magnetic metal jelly roll pan on which students can manipulate the letters. Have students practice spelling each of the new sight words. After students have practiced with the magnetic letters, hold a class spelling bee. As you call on students to spell the new sight words, allow them to use the magnetic letters for reference. After students have shown that they know the new words, include the other sight words they have learned so far.

Play It

I'm Thinking of a Word . . .

Play *I'm Thinking of a Word* with students. Post the new sight words for students to see. Start by saying, "I'm thinking of a word that . . ." and then complete the sentence with various hints. You might give clues about the word's first or last letter, name words that rhyme with the chosen word, list words that have the same meaning, and so on. After you have challenged each student, give volunteers an opportunity to test the class with their own *I'm Thinking of a Word* clues.

3 Under here.

2 Where?

FOLD #1

4 I am not so blue!

Read It Mini-Book

Sight Words:
blue, come, under, where

FOLD #2

Blue, come here! 1

Review It Comic Strip

See It

Trace the word "see."

see see

see see

Print the word "at" four times.

Connect the letters to make the word "brown."

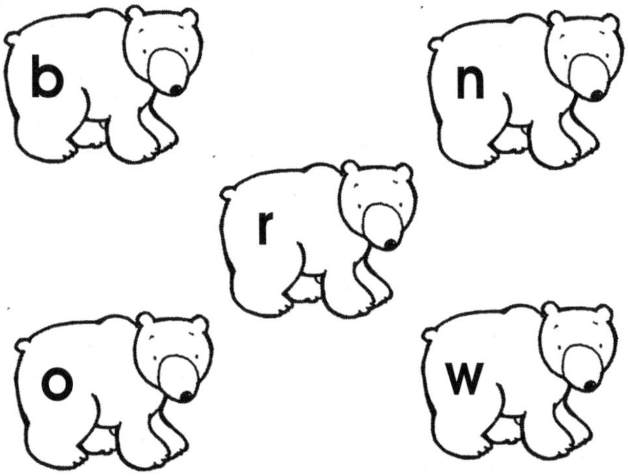

b n

r

o w

Color each letter to make the word "red."

red

Find It

Cross out the word in each row that does not belong.

brown	brown	brown	crown	brown
red	red	red	read	red
see	see	see	see	sea
at	ant	at	at	at

Name: _____

Directions: Read the story written by Bill Martin, *Brown Bear, Brown Bear, What Do You See?*
(Henry Holt and Co. ©1996). Then, cut out and paste the pictures to complete the story.

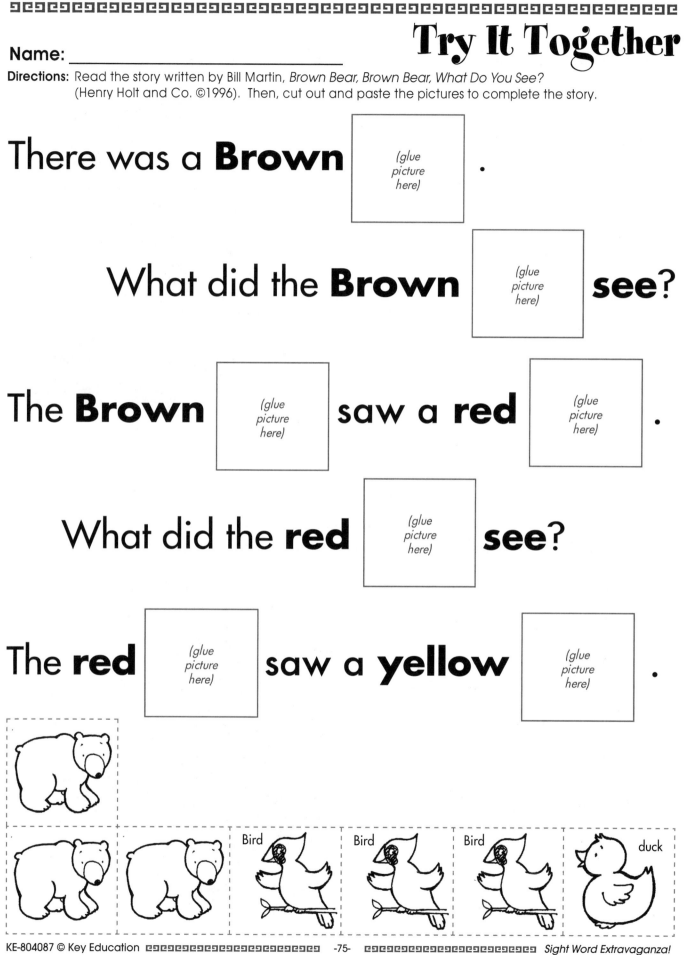

There was a **Brown** *(glue picture here)* .

What did the **Brown** *(glue picture here)* **see**?

The **Brown** *(glue picture here)* saw a **red** *(glue picture here)* .

What did the **red** *(glue picture here)* **see**?

The **red** *(glue picture here)* saw a **yellow** *(glue picture here)* .

Bird   Bird   Bird   duck

Do It

Sight Word Matching

Use a die cutout to make sets of the new sight words so that each student will have a piece of paper from which the words have been cut and a set of the cutout letters in another color. (Choose two contrasting colors of paper, such as black and white or blue and yellow.) Give a cutout sight words paper and the letters to each student. Allow students to practice spelling the new sight words by matching the paper letters to the puzzle-like word papers. Then, collect the word papers so that students can use the letters to make the words on their own.

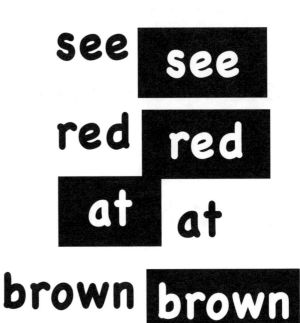

Play It

Brown Bear, Brown Bear

Read aloud the book *Brown Bear, Brown Bear, What Do You See?* by Bill Martin, Jr. to the class. Add some extra fun and test your students' recognition of the new sight words by rereading the book and having them stand up (and quickly sit) each time you read one of the new sight words. Remind them that they will have to listen closely to catch all of the words. For example:

Brown *(stand)* **Bear,**

Brown *(stand)* **Bear,**

What do you <u>see</u>? *(stand)*

I <u>see</u> *(stand)* **a <u>red</u>** *(stand)* **bird**

Looking <u>at</u> *(stand)* **me.**

<u>Red</u> *(stand)* **Bird,**

<u>Red</u> *(stand)* **Bird,**

What do you <u>see</u>? *(stand)*

I <u>see</u> *(stand)* **a yellow duck**

Looking <u>at</u> *(stand)* **me.**

FOLD #1

Read It Mini-Book

Sight Words:
at, brown, red, see

FOLD #2

4

At last!

1

I see red.

Review It Comic Strip

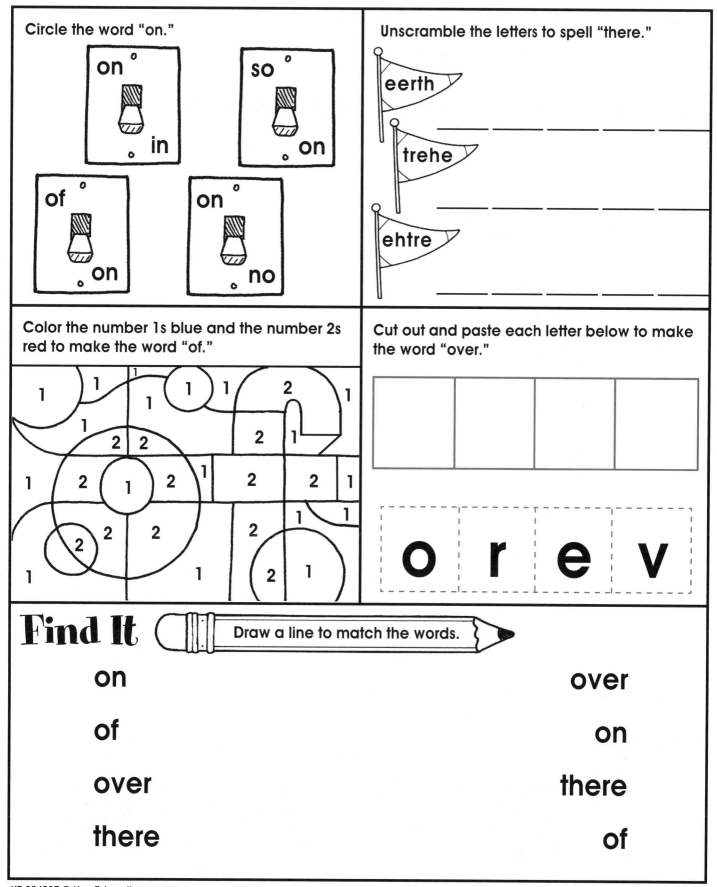

Circle the word "on."

on   o
in

so   o
on

of   o
on

on   o
no

Unscramble the letters to spell "there."

eerth _____

trehe _____

_____

ehtre _____

Color the number 1s blue and the number 2s red to make the word "of."

Cut out and paste each letter below to make the word "over."

o   r   e   v

Find It

Draw a line to match the words.

on   over

of   on

over   there

there   of

Name: _____

Directions: Read the story written by Margaret Wise Brown, *Goodnight Moon* (HarperCollins ©1991). Then, cut out and paste the pictures to complete the story.

In the green room **there** was a [glue picture here] .

And a red [glue picture here] .

And a picture **of** the [glue picture here] jumping

over the [glue picture here] .

There were [glue picture here] little [glue picture here]

sitting **on** [glue picture here] .

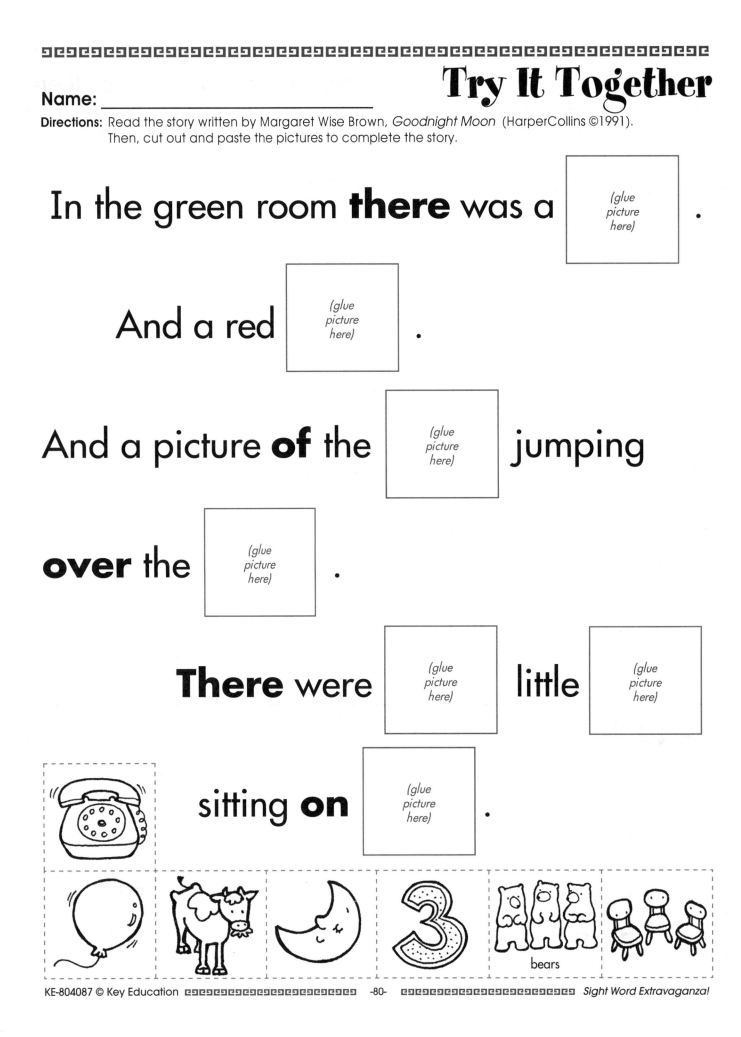

bears

Do It

Sign Language Finger Spelling

Teach students how to spell each of the new sight words using the American Sign Language alphabet. This is not only a fun and tactile way to learn, but it also encourages learning another language.

Play It

Fill in the Blanks

Explain that the new sight words sometimes have a similar job. Each can indicate placement or give a hint about where something is. On chart paper, write the following sentences:

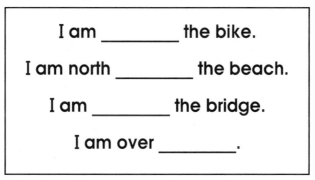

I am _____ the bike.

I am north _____ the beach.

I am _____ the bridge.

I am over _____.

Then, have students suggest as a class which new sight word should go in each blank. (The answers in order: *on*, *of*, *over* or *on*, *there*.) To follow up, provide students with several clues using similar sentences about an object in the room. For example, to describe the classroom alphabet strip, you might say:

I am <u>on</u> the board.

I am north <u>of</u> the chalk tray.

I am <u>over</u> the writing.

Ask a student volunteer to point to the object and guess its identity by saying, "I am over <u>there</u>." Invite students to describe the position of other classroom objects while focusing on the new sight words.

Both of them
are there.

FOLD #1

He is over.

Read It Mini-Book

Sight Words:
of, on, over, there

Both are over!

FOLD #2

She is on.

Review It Comic Strip

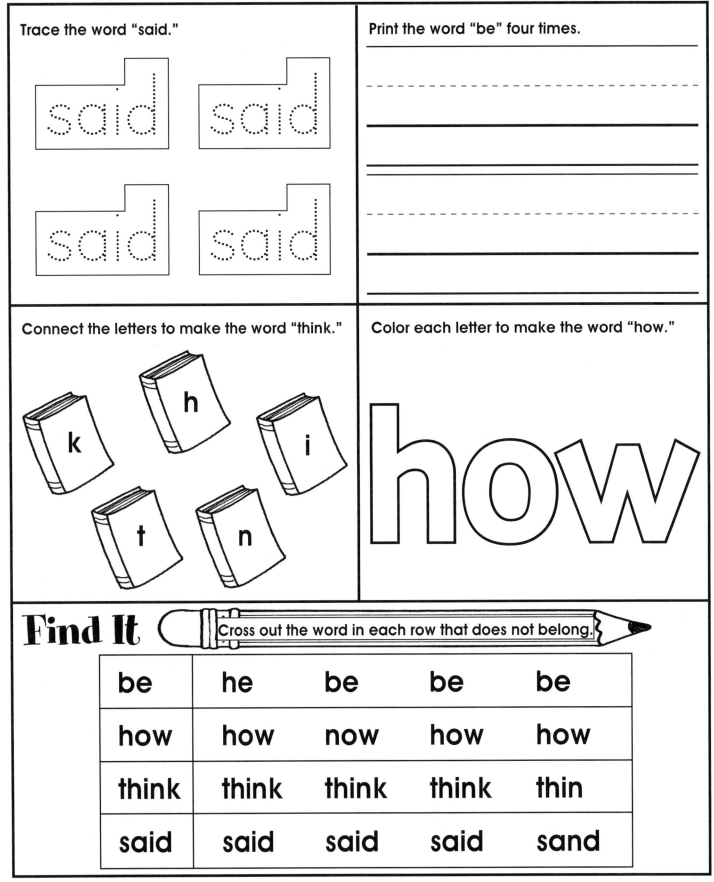

Trace the word "said."

said   said

said   said

Print the word "be" four times.

Connect the letters to make the word "think."

k   h   i

t   n

Color each letter to make the word "how."

how

Find It

Cross out the word in each row that does not belong.

be	he	be	be	be
how	how	now	how	how
think	think	think	think	thin
said	said	said	said	sand

Try It Together

Name: _____

Directions: Read the story written by Sam McBratney, *Guess How Much I Love You*
(Candlewick Press ©1995). Then, cut out and paste the pictures to complete the story.

Big Nutbrown *(glue picture here)* was listening.

Little Nutbrown *(glue picture here)* **said**,

"Guess **how** much *(glue picture here)* *(glue picture here)* you."

Big Nutbrown *(glue picture here)* **said**, "Oh, *(glue picture here)*

don't **think** *(glue picture here)* could guess that."

They *(glue picture here)* each other to **be** sure.

Hare

Hare   Hare

• • • • • • • • • • • • • • Do It • • • • • • • • • • • • • •

Guess How Much I Love You

Read aloud the book *Guess How Much I Love You* by Sam McBratney. Return the students' papers from the Try It Together activity (page 85). Have students review their work and then circle all of the sight words in the passage that they have learned. Students may practice writing the sight words on the backs of their papers.

He wanted to be sure that

Big Nutbrown Hare was listening.

"Guess how much I love you," he said.

"Oh, I don't think I could guess that,"

said Big Nutbrown Hare.

List of Sight Words in Preceding Chapters				
all	could	I	play	to
and	do	in	put	under
are	down	is	red	up
at	find	it	said	was
away	for	know	see	we
be	get	like	she	went
blue	go	little	so	what
boy	had	me	that	when
brown	has	my	the	where
but	have	not	them	who
by	he	of	there	will
came	her	on	think	with
come	how	one	this	yes
		over	three	you

• • • • • • • • • • • • • Play It • • • • • • • • • • • • •

Beach Ball Word Toss

Have students sit in a circle. Post the new sight words for all to see. Begin by allowing students to toss a beach ball to one another. Explain that as each of them tosses the ball, that student must say one of the new sight words. If a student stumbles on a word or misses the ball, restart the toss. Guide the toss by starting slowly and then gradually speeding it up. Then, slow the toss down again to be sure all students are ready and listening. Next, post a list of all of the sight words students have learned (see above). Play beach ball word toss until all of the sight words have been said at least once.

☆3
"How?" she said.

"How could it be?" ☆2

FOLD #1

Read It Mini-Book

Sight Words:
be, how, said, think

☆4 That is how.

FOLD #2

"Think," she said. ☆1

Review It Comic Strip

New Words: ate, look, out, some

Circle the word "ate."

Unscramble the letters to spell "look."

olok ___ ___ ___ ___

kool ___ ___ ___ ___

oklo ___ ___ ___ ___

Color the number 1s blue and the number 2s red to make the word "out."

Cut out and paste each letter below to make the word "some."

e   o   s   m

Find It

Draw a line to match the words.

look   ate

ate   out

out   some

some   look

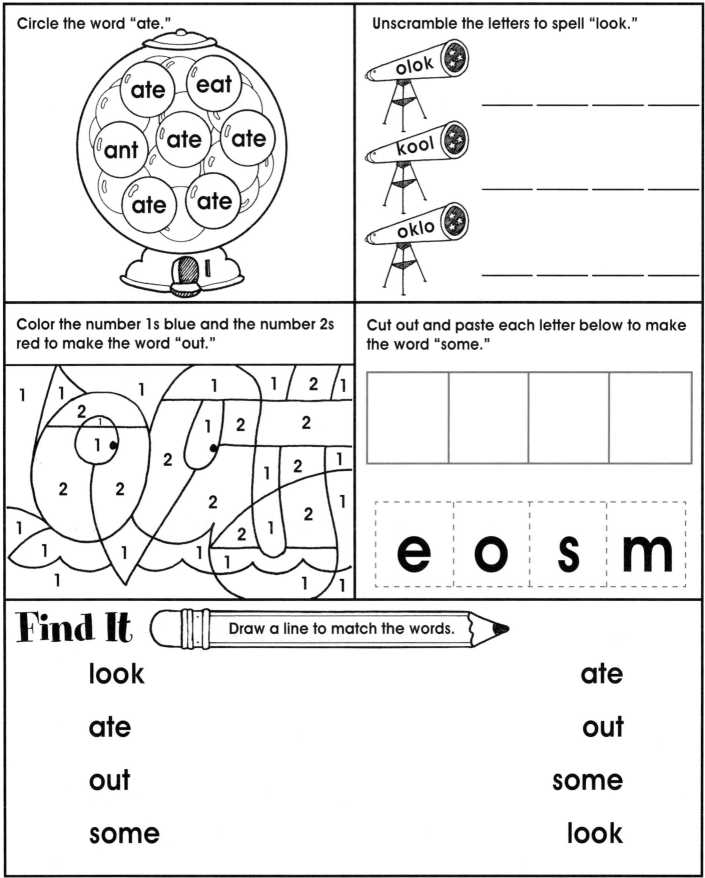

Name: _____

Directions: Read the story written by Eric Carle, *The Very Hungry Caterpillar*
(Philomel ©1994). Then, cut out and paste the pictures to complete the story.

There was a little [(glue picture here)] on a [(glue picture here)] .

One morning the [(glue picture here)] came up.

A tiny and very hungry [(glue picture here)]

popped **out** of the [(glue picture here)] .

The [(glue picture here)] went to **look** for **some** food.

He **ate** one [(glue picture here)] and was still hungry.

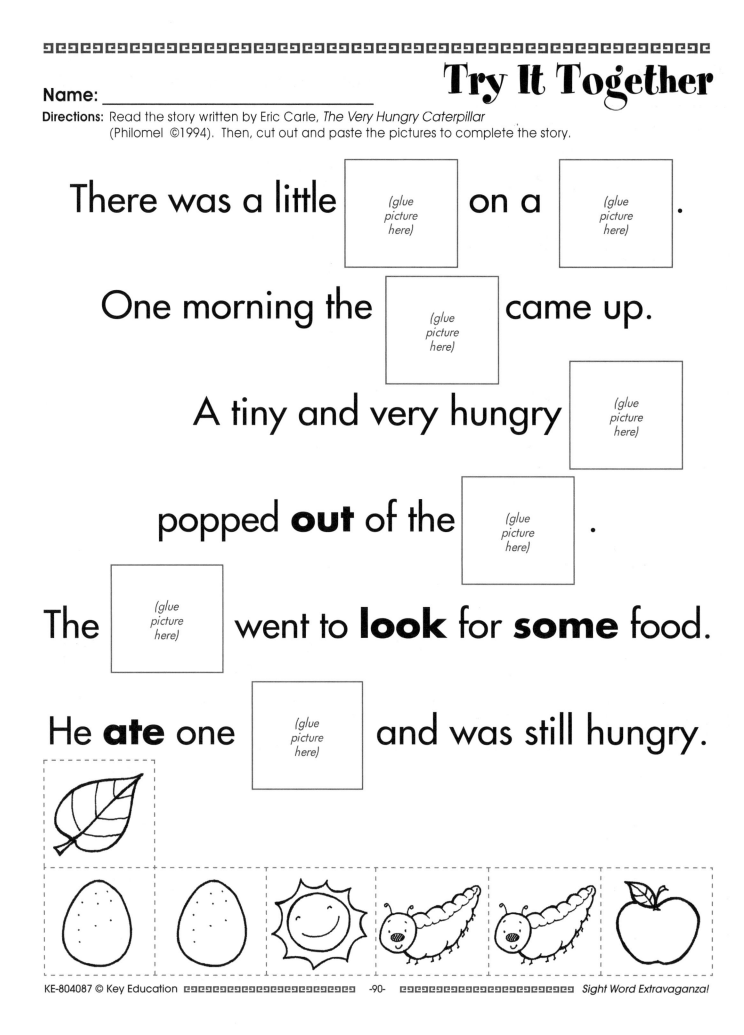

Do It

Spelling Circles

Provide each student with 14 paper circles in various colors, approximately 5" (12.7 cm) in diameter. Instruct students to write the letters from each new sight word on their paper circles, one letter per circle. Then, have students reorganize their paper circles to spell out each word. Have them overlap the circles slightly and glue them together to form each of the four new sight words. Collect the students' paper circle words and arrange them in four different word caterpillar groups around the room. Title the display "Hungry for Words."

Play It

Hot Potato Spelling

Have students sit in a circle to play a version of Hot Potato. Select one of the new sight words as the "hot potato" word. As students toss a beanbag or other soft object to each other, play some quiet but lively music. Then, stop the music suddenly and say the hot potato word. Whoever is left holding the beanbag when the sight word is said must spell the word on the board for everyone to see. If you know that a student will need help, offer clues or allow the student to choose a partner for assistance. Play several rounds of the game, naming a new sight word for each round, till all of the sight words have been said and spelled several times.

3

You ate some?

I ate some.

2

FOLD #1

4

I ate some.

FOLD #2

Read It Mini-Book

Sight Words:
ate, look, out, some

Look out!

1

Review It Comic Strip

See It

Trace the word "here."

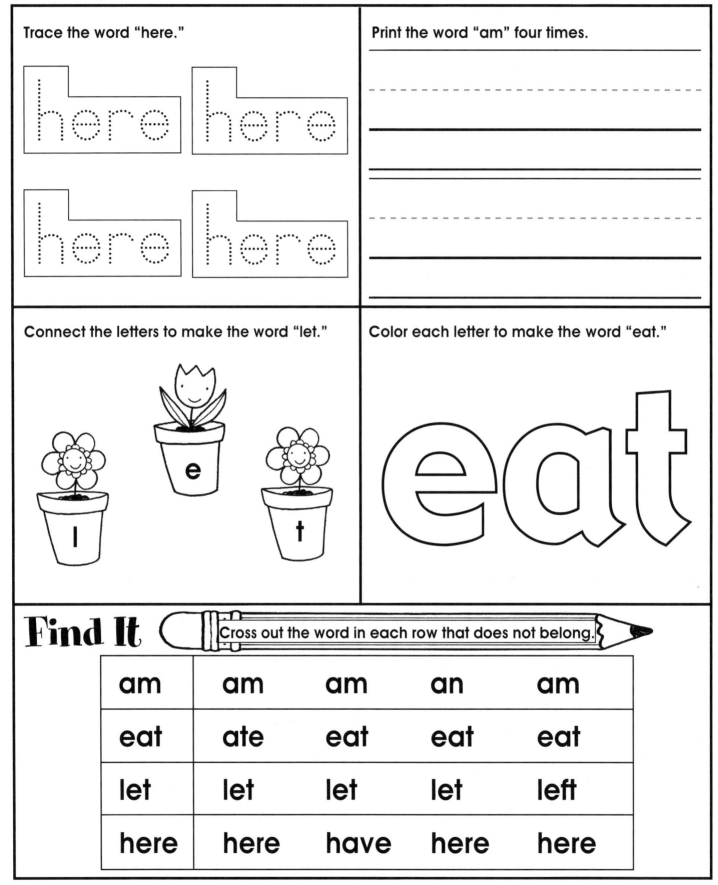

Print the word "am" four times.

Connect the letters to make the word "let."

Color each letter to make the word "eat."

Find It

Cross out the word in each row that does not belong.

am	am	am	an	am
eat	ate	eat	eat	eat
let	let	let	let	left
here	here	have	here	here

Name: _____

Directions: Read the story written by Dr. Seuss, *Green Eggs and Ham* (Random House Books for Young Readers ©1960). Then, cut out and paste the pictures to complete the story.

Sam-I-**am** let him **be**!

He will not **eat** green [glue picture here] and ham.

He will not **eat** them with a [glue picture here] .

He will not **eat** them in a [glue picture here] .

He will not **eat** them with a [glue picture here] .

He will not **eat** them in a [glue picture here] .

He will not **eat** them **here** or there.
He will not **eat** them anywhere!

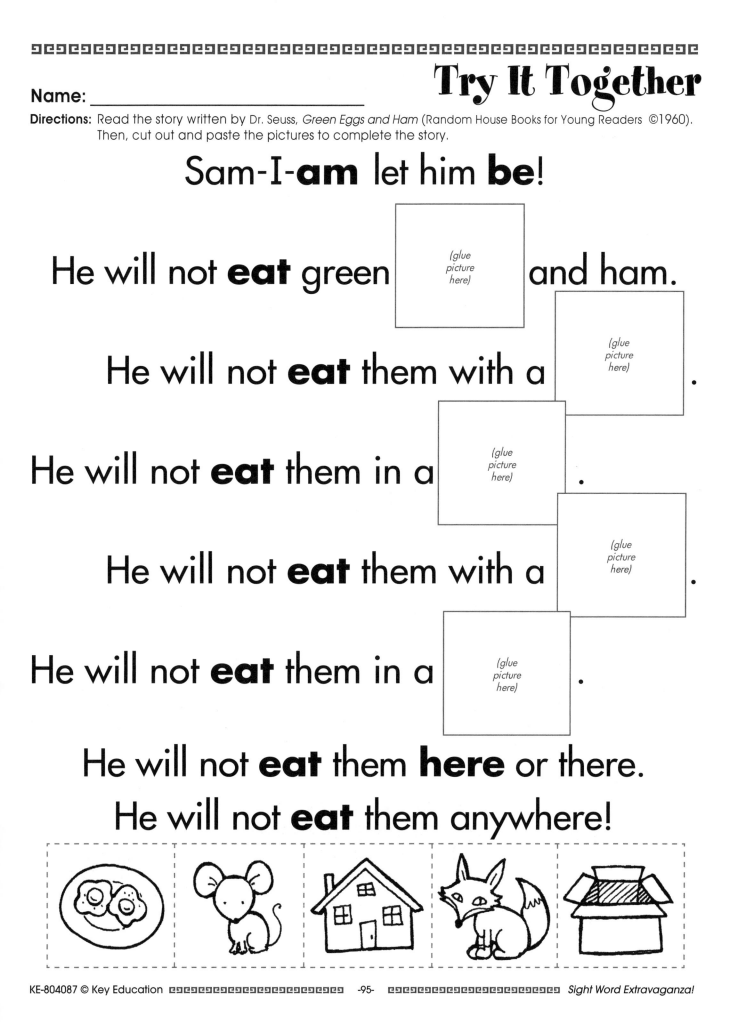

. . . . Do It . . . .

Rhyme Time

Have students work on their rhyming skills while practicing the new sight words. First, set up four tables, one for each sight word. Add visual rhyming cues by arranging picture cards and displaying several objects on each table. Distribute writing paper and instruct students to write the four sight words across the top of their papers. Then, have them list all of the words they can think of that rhyme with each word (spelling the words the best they can). See the following examples:

am	eat	let	here
ham	beet	jet	cheer
Sam	feet	net	deer
clam	meat	pet	year
jam	sweet	vet	steer
lamb	treat	wet	tear
ram	wheat	sweat	fear

. . . . Play It . . . .

Doggy, Doggy, Where's Your Bone?

Have students play the game *Doggy, Doggy, Where's Your Bone?* but with a special rhyme (see below) to reinforce the new sight words. Write the rhyme on the board or post it on chart paper for all students to see. Highlight the new sight words so that students will emphasize them when they are said. As a class, go over the rhyme several times before playing the game. To play, choose a student to begin as the doggy. The doggy sits in a chair at the front of the room with eyes closed and facing away from the class. Place a small object—the bone—under the doggy's chair. Silently point to another student who creeps up behind the doggy, steals the bone, and returns to his seat, concealing the bone. The class chants the rhyme and the doggy has three guesses to name the student who took the bone. If the doggy guesses correctly, she gets another turn as the doggy. If not, the student with the bone becomes the new doggy.

Doggy, Doggy, <u>here</u> is your bone!
I just stole it from your home.
<u>Let</u> me <u>eat</u> it all alone.
Try to find it.
I <u>am</u> unknown.

KE-804087 © Key Education   -97-   Sight Word Extravaganza!

I am here.

Let me eat!

★1

★4

Read It Mini-Book

Sight Words:
am, eat, here, let

Let me eat.

I am here!

★2

★3

Review It Comic Strip

See It

New Words: ask, give, make, want

Circle the word "ask."

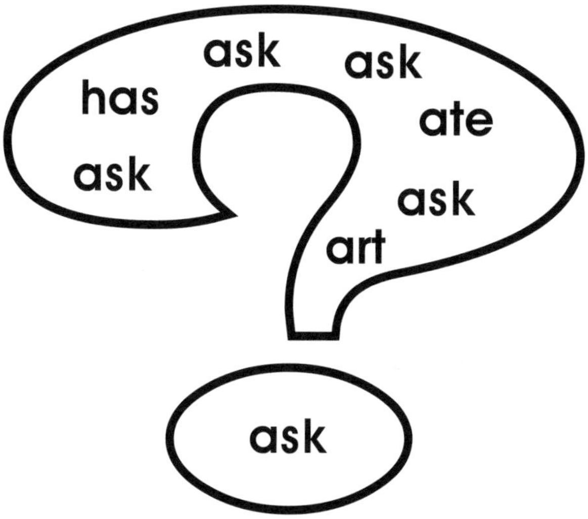
ask
ask
has
ate
ask
ask
art
ask

Unscramble the letters to spell "make."

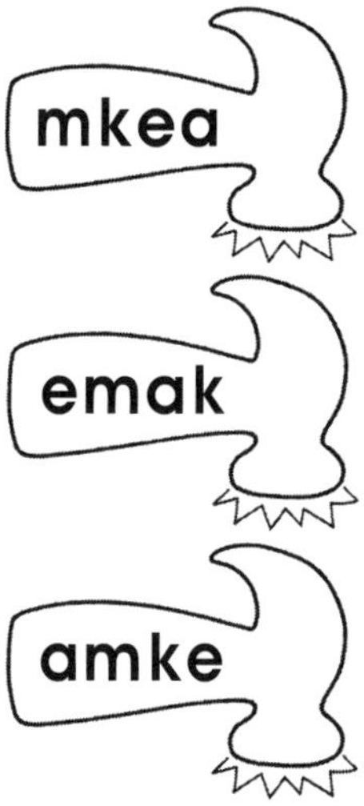
mkea
emak
amke

Color the number 1s blue and the number 2s red to make the word "give."

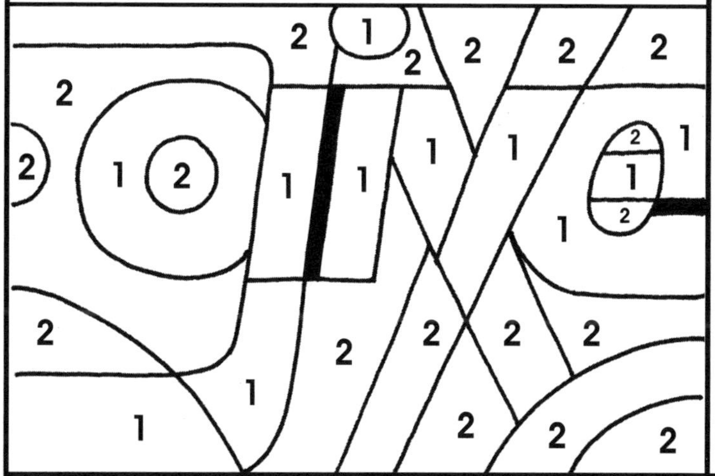

Cut out and paste each letter below to make the word "want."

t	w	a	n

Find It

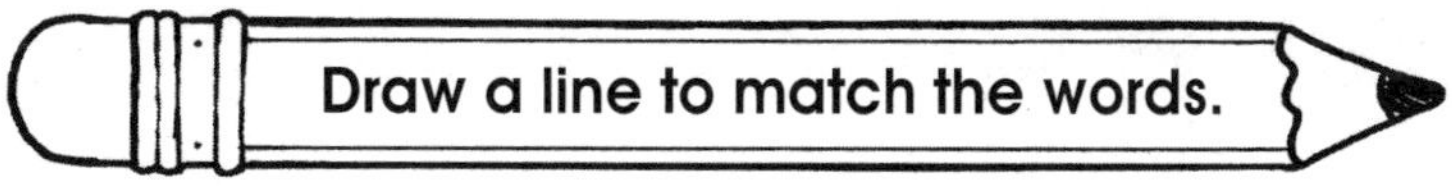
Draw a line to match the words.

make	give
want	ask
give	make
ask	want

Name: _____

Directions: Read the story written by Laura Joffe Numeroff, *If You Give a Mouse a Cookie* (HarperCollins ©1985). Then, cut out and paste the pictures to complete the story.

When the *(glue picture here)* eats a *(glue picture here)* ,

he will **ask** you for a glass of *(glue picture here)* .

If you **give** him the *(glue picture here)* ,

then he will **ask** you for a *(glue picture here)* .

Next he will **need** a *(glue picture here)* .

Then, he will **want** to look in a *(glue picture here)* .

to **make** sure he is not messy.

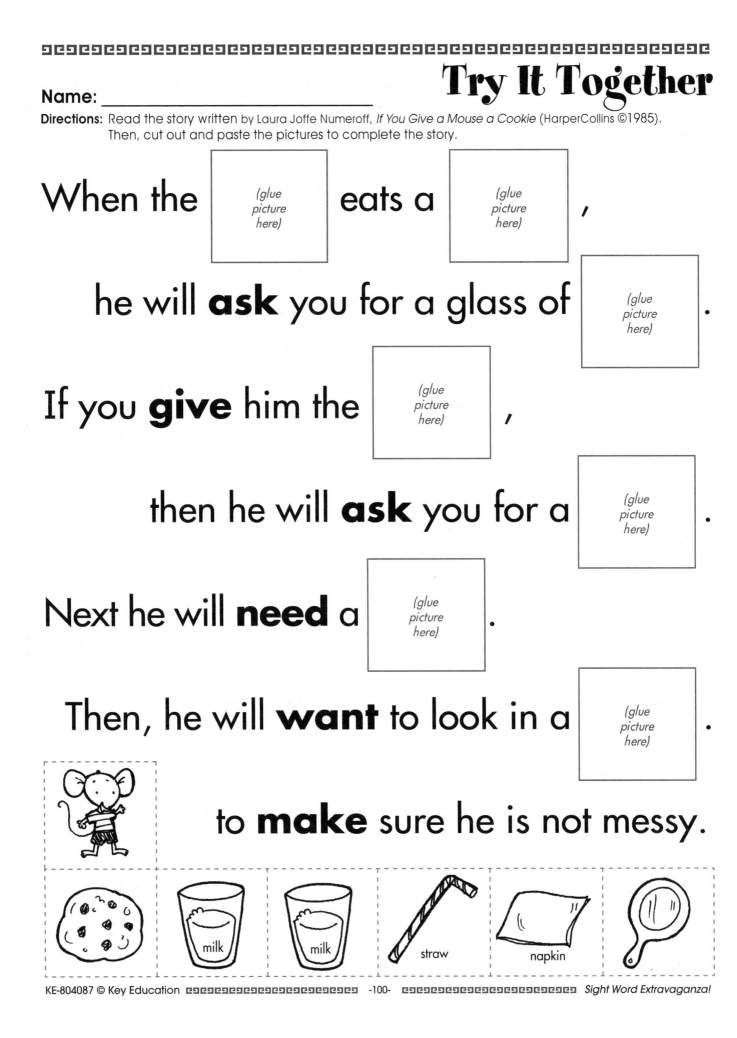

milk

milk

straw

napkin

Do It

Sight Word Book Search

Divide students into pairs. Provide each pair with a piece of lined paper and one of the books from the If You Give . . . book series by Laura Joffe Numeroff: *If You Give a Mouse a Cookie*, *If You Give a Moose a Muffin*, *If You Give a Pig a Pancake*, *If You Take a Mouse to School*, *If You Give a Pig a Party*, *If You Take a Mouse to the Movies*, and *If You Give a Cat a Cupcake*. Be sure that at least two pairs of students have the same book. Display the new sight words. Instruct students to fold their papers in half vertically and write "Sight Word" at the top of the paper on the left side and "Page" on the right side.

Have the student pairs work together to find the new sight words in their books and record each word and its page number on their papers. When they are done, have the pairs that read the same book compare their work to make sure they found all of the words. To extend the activity, have students look in their books for all of the sight words the class has been studying.

Play It

More Verbs

Explain to students that all four new sight words are special words called verbs, words that may show activity, just like the previously learned words *could, get, go,* and *went* (see page 49). Demonstrate how to use each verb in a different sentence to create a silly short story. First, post the new sight words. Then, on chart paper, write a silly sentence with one of the words to get the story started. Ask students to offer ideas for other sentences. See the following sample story:

Teacher sentence: I <u>make</u> purple pancakes.
Student sentence: The aliens <u>want</u> some.
Student sentence: "<u>Give</u> us more!" they said.
Student sentence: "<u>Ask</u> nicely," I said.

☆3 Ask me.

FOLD #1

☆2 Give it.

☆4 Make me!

Read It Mini-Book

Sight Words:
ask, give, make, want

FOLD #2

Want it. ☆1

KE-804087 © Key Education   -102-   *Sight Word Extravaganza!*

Review It Comic Strip

Trace the word "now."

now now

now now

Print the word "please" two times.

Connect the letters to make the word "just."

u

s

t

j

Color each letter to make the word "can."

can

Find It

Cross out the word in each row that does not belong.

can	can	ran	can	can
now	now	now	new	now
please	pause	please	please	please
just	just	just	just	jest

Try It Together

Name: _____

Directions: Read the story written by Laura Joffe Numeroff, *Marvin K. Mooney, Will You Please Go Now!* (Random House Books for Young Readers ©1972). Then, cut out and paste the pictures to complete the story.

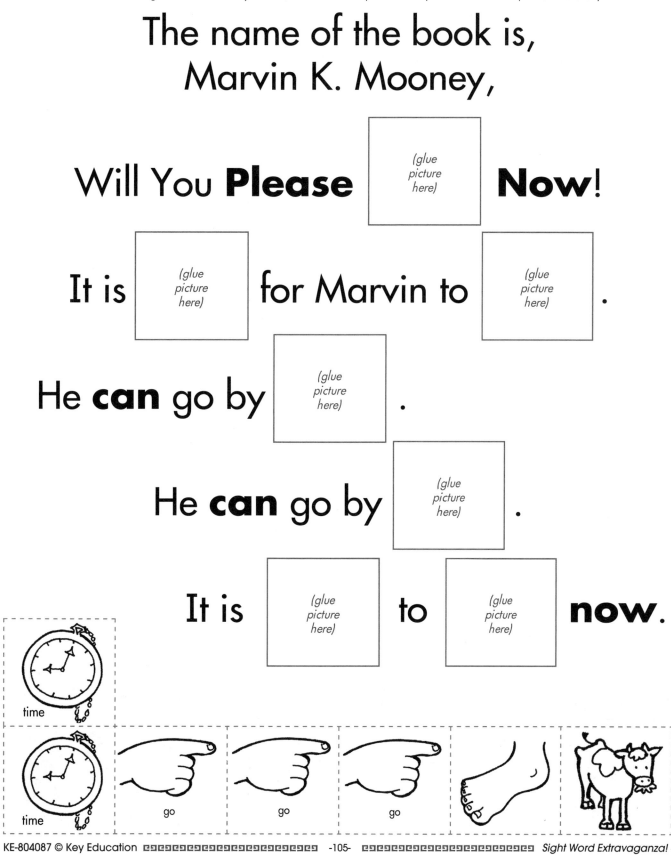

The name of the book is,
Marvin K. Mooney,

Will You **Please** (glue picture here) **Now**!

It is (glue picture here) for Marvin to (glue picture here) .

He **can** go by (glue picture here) .

He **can** go by (glue picture here) .

It is (glue picture here) to (glue picture here) **now**.

time

time   go   go   go

Do It

Make Goopy Words

Make four batches of fun goo. For each batch, mix together in a large bowl one 16 oz. box of cornstarch, about 1.5 cups (355 mL) of water, and 12 drops of food coloring, using a different color for each batch. Cover four tables with old sheets or plastic tablecloths. On each table, place one bowl of fun goo, a big plastic cup for scooping, a large cookie sheet, an apron, and a word card labeled with one of the new sight words. Allow students to take turns wearing an apron (this stuff is fun but a little messy) and plopping a scoop of the fun goo on the cookie sheet. Students can then use a finger to practice writing the table's featured sight word in the goo. They'll enjoy spelling the words and then watching them "disappear" after each word is written.

Play It

Mother, May I?

Play *Mother, May I?* as a class. Change the wording in the game to reinforce the new sight words. Post the phrases on the board or chart paper for students to see, highlighting the new words so that they stand out. For example:

Mother command: "Maggie, take five giant steps forward."
Player response: "Mother, may I? I <u>can</u> <u>now</u>? <u>Please</u> <u>just</u> let me. Do you allow?"
Mother command: "Maggie, you <u>can</u> <u>now</u>. You said <u>please</u>, so <u>just</u> go right <u>now</u>."

Sight Word Extravaganza!

Read It Mini-Book

Can I?

1

Sight Words:
can, just, now, please

FOLD #2

Please, just eat.

4

2 Can I now?

Please, can I just eat? **3**

FOLD #1

Review It Comic Strip

Circle the word "they."

Unscramble the letters to spell "say."

a y s _____ _____ _____

y s a _____ _____ _____

a s y _____ _____ _____

Color the number 1s blue and the number 2s red to make the word "good."

Cut out and paste each letter below to make the word "from."

o   r   m   f

Find It

Draw a line to match the words.

they   say

say   from

good   they

from   good

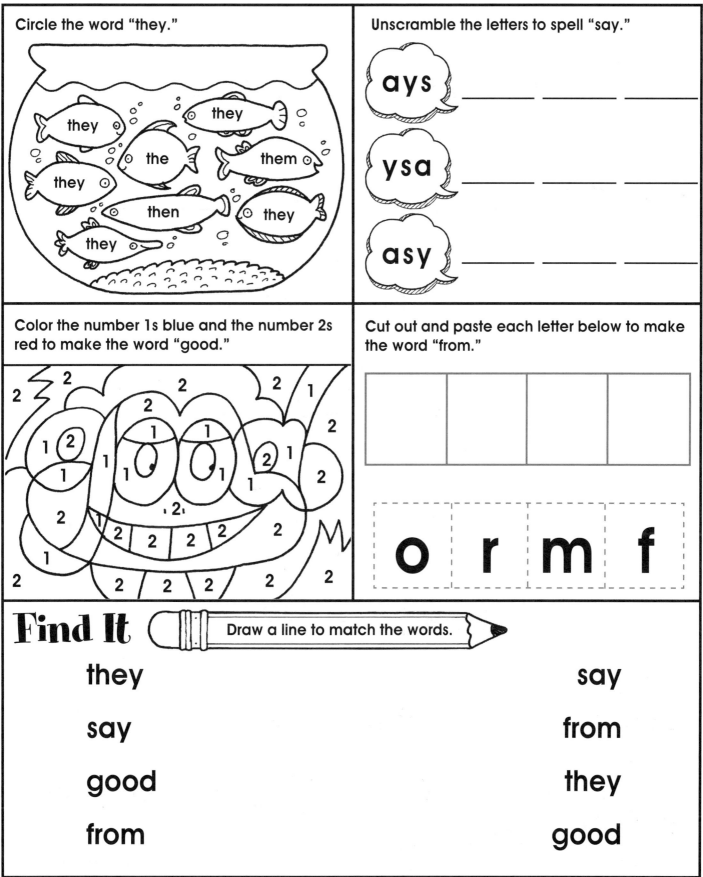

Name: _____

Directions: Read the story written by Jane Yolen, *How Do Dinosaurs Say Good Night?* (Blue Sky Press © 2000). Then, cut out and paste the pictures to complete the story.

How do you think [glue picture here] **say good** night?

Does the [glue picture here] come in and

turn off the [glue picture here] ?

Do [glue picture here] swing their [glue picture here] **from**

side to side?

Do **they** [glue picture here] ?

Or do **they** want [glue picture here] rides?

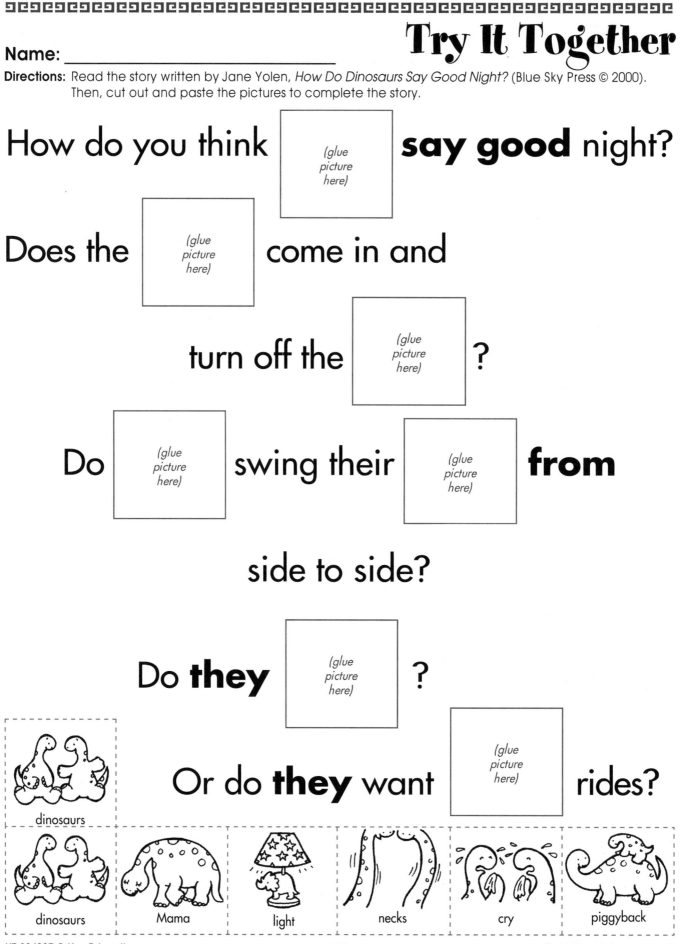

dinosaurs

dinosaurs   Mama   light   necks   cry   piggyback

Do It

Fishing for Letters

Set a plastic tub or other large, deep container in the corner of the room. Inside the tub, place all of the magnetic letters needed to spell the new sight words: *a, d, e, f, g, h, m, o, o, r, s, t, y*. Mix the letters with shredded paper or packing peanuts. Attach a magnet to the string of a toy fishing rod (or make a simple one by tying the magnet and yarn to the end of a flexible stick). Allow students to take turns fishing the letters out of the tub and making each of the new sight words.

Play It

Letter Shopping

Fill a large paper grocery bag with alphabet cards that include the letters needed to make all of the new sight words at the same time: *a, d, e, f, g, h, m, o, o, o, r, s, t, y, y*. Place the bag on the floor at the front of the room. Have student shoppers take turns picking out a letter card and holding it up for all to see. Encourage students to point out when a letter from one of the new sight words has been chosen. Post those sight word letters and have students add to them to build the words. Play until each new sight word has been spelled.

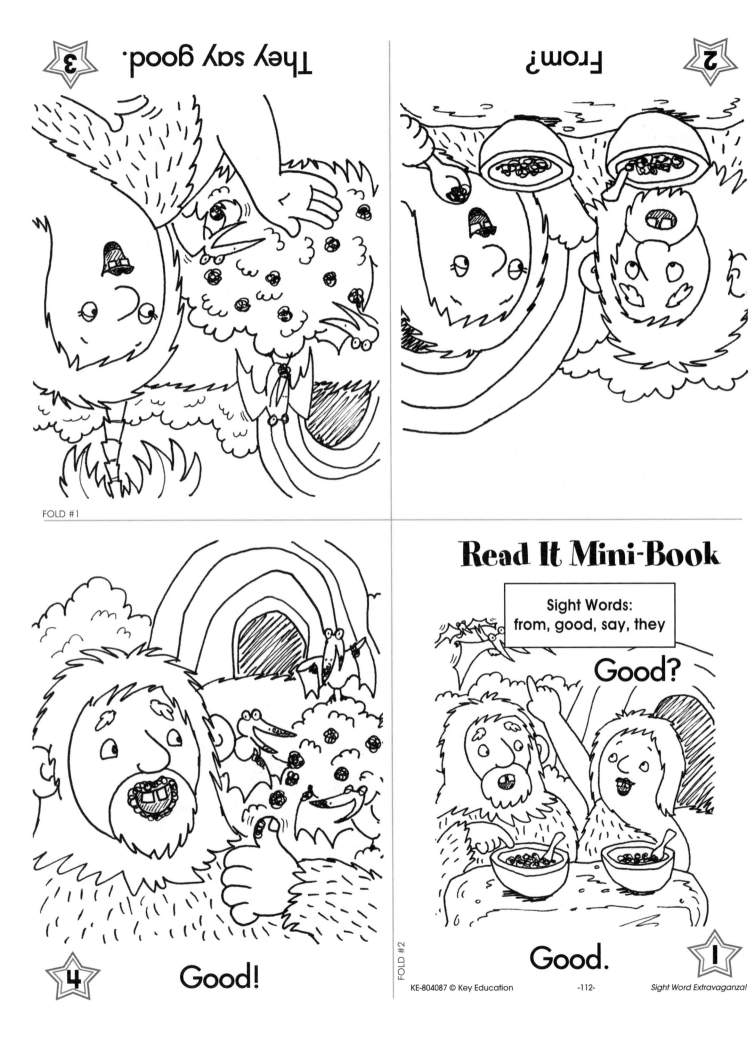

They say good.

3

From?

2

FOLD #1

Good!

4

Read It Mini-Book

Sight Words:
from, good, say, they

Good?

FOLD #2

Good.

1

Review It Comic Strip

See It

New Words: big, him, no, thank

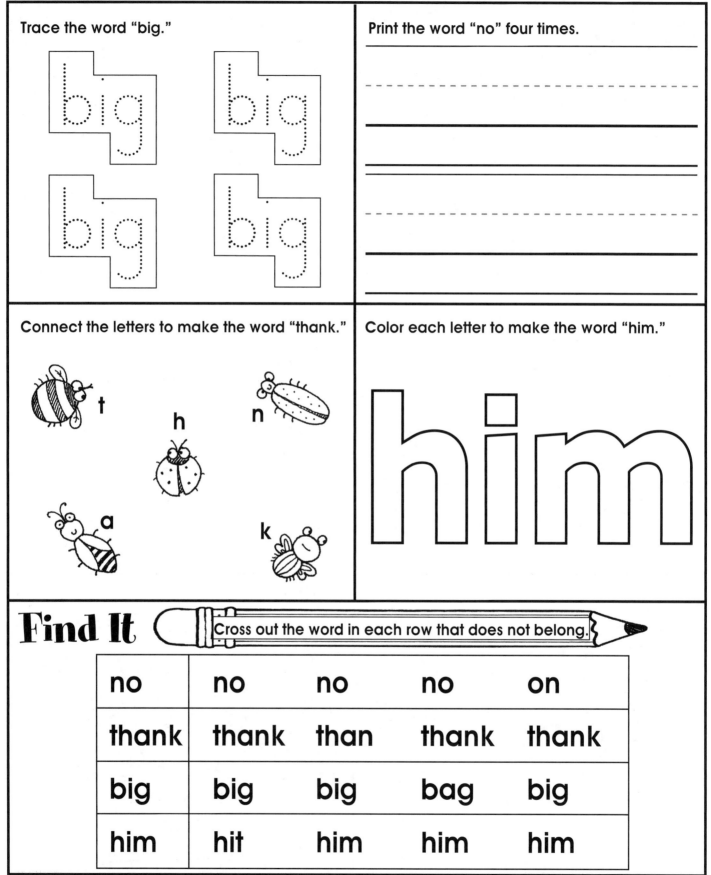

Trace the word "big."

Print the word "no" four times.

Connect the letters to make the word "thank."

t h n a k

Color each letter to make the word "him."

him

Find It

Cross out the word in each row that does not belong.

no	no	no	no	on
thank	thank	than	thank	thank
big	big	big	bag	big
him	hit	him	him	him

Try It Together

Directions: Read the story written by Jane Yolen, *How Do Dinosaurs Eat Their Food?* (Blue Sky Press © 2005). Then, cut out and paste the pictures to complete the story.

How does a **big** *(glue picture here)* like to eat?

Does he eat *(glue picture here)* ? Does he eat *(glue picture here)* ?

Does he drink his *(glue picture here)* ?

Does he squeeze juicy *(glue picture here)* ?

He says, "Please" and "**No thank** you."

The *(glue picture here)* eats all the food given to **him**.

dinosaur   dinosaur   broccoli   beans   milk   oranges

Do It

Sweet Sight Words

Place four different colored tubes of cake decorating icing at four different tables and give each student a paper plate. Allow students to write each new sight word on their paper plates in icing. After all of the students have written the new sight words, present each of them with a real cupcake. Let students use icing to decorate the cupcakes and then enjoy their sweet treats. Caution: Before completing any food activity, ask families' permission and inquire about students' food allergies and religious or other food preferences.

Play It

Sight Word Speed Reading

Provide each student with four index cards and a marker. Instruct students to use their neatest handwriting to write each of the new sight words on a separate card. (Alternatively, use the cards provided on pages 154–159.) Divide the class into groups of three. Have each group pick one person to hold the cards; the other two students will be players. Explain that the card holder will display the 12 word cards like flashcards and the two players will see who can be first to recognize and name each word as it is shown. Have the students in the groups change roles so that each student has a chance to hold and flash the cards.

☆ 3

¡Big?

FOLD #1

☆ 2 No, thank you. Big!

Read It Mini-Book

Sight Words:
big, him, no, thank

☆ 4

Big.

FOLD #2

Him?

☆ 1

Review It Comic Strip

See It

Circle the word "saw."

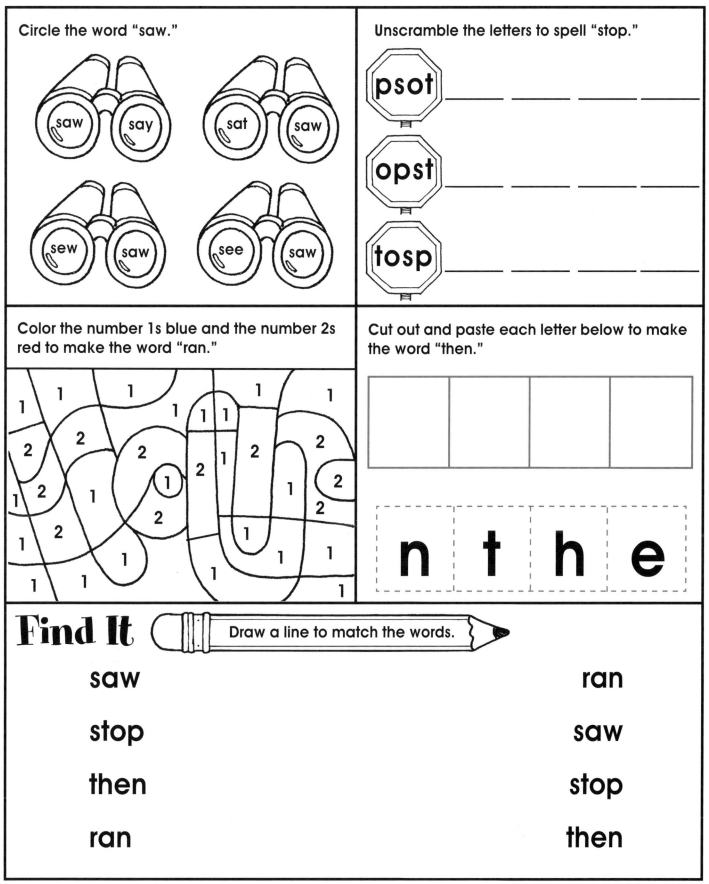

Unscramble the letters to spell "stop."

psot _____ _____ _____ _____

opst _____ _____ _____ _____

tosp _____ _____ _____ _____

Color the number 1s blue and the number 2s red to make the word "ran."

Cut out and paste each letter below to make the word "then."

n   t   h   e

Find It

Draw a line to match the words.

saw	ran
stop	saw
then	stop
ran	then

Name: _____

Directions: Read the story written by P. D. Eastman, *Are You My Mother?* (Random House © 1995). Then, cut out and paste the pictures to complete the story.

The baby [(glue picture here)] looked [(glue picture here)] .

He **saw** a big [(glue picture here)] [(glue picture here)] in the sky.

He said, "There she is!"

"There is my [(glue picture here)] !"

He **ran**. The [(glue picture here)] did not **stop**.

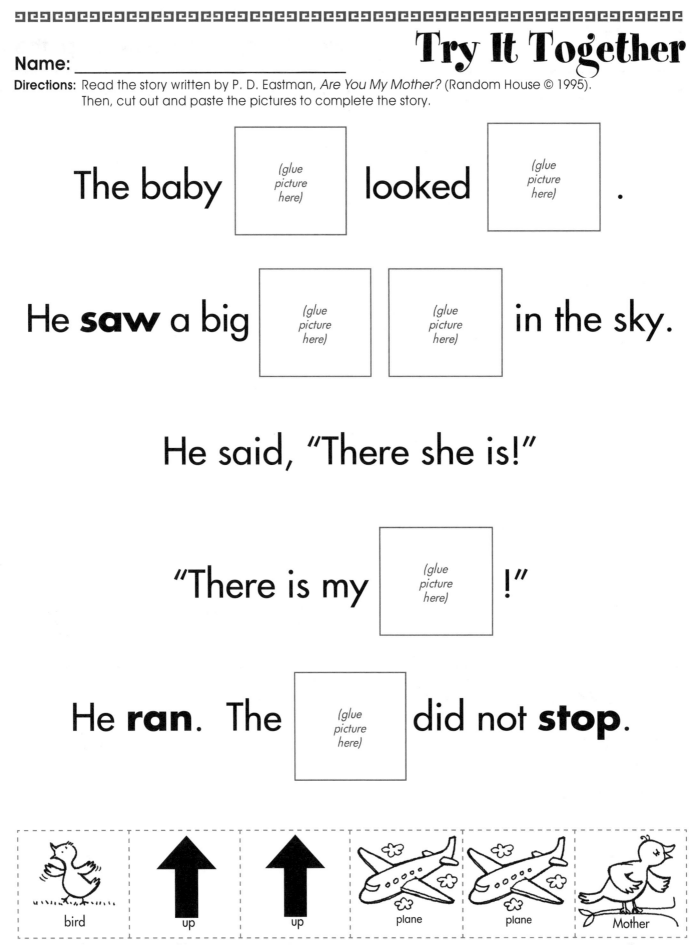

bird

up

up

plane

plane

Mother

Do It

Stampin' Sight Words

Cover four tables with old sheets or plastic tablecloths. Make four colorful "ink" pads by placing folded paper towels in pie tins and soaking them with nontoxic paint. On each table, place a word card with one of the new sight words, a set of foam bathtub letters that spell the sight word, a stack of drawing paper, a prepared pie tin of paint, and a paint smock or an old, large T-shirt. Allow students to take turns putting on the smock, pressing each letter onto the paint pad, and stamping the letters on a piece of drawing paper to "write" the sight word. After students have had a chance to make each of the words, allow their papers to dry and post them on a display titled "Stampin' Sight Words."

Play It

Sight Word Go Fish

Provide each student with four index cards and a marker. Instruct students to neatly write one of the new sight words on each card. (Alternatively, use the cards provided on pages 154–159.) Divide the class into groups of three or four. Allow each group to play a variation of the card game Go Fish. First, students in each group should place their word cards in a stack. Have one student deal the cards to each player, including himself. The object is for each player to try to collect all three (or four) of the same word card by asking the other players for certain words. For example, a player might say, "Mason, do you have any *stops*?" If the player receives the requested card or cards, she continues her turn with another question. Play proceeds until all sets of the four new sight word cards have been collected.

Then, I ran.

I had to stop.

FOLD #1

Read It Mini-Book

Sight Words:
ran, saw, stop, then

4

I

I saw it.

Review It Comic Strip

Trace the word "black."

black black

black black

Print the word "every" two times.

Connect the letters to make the word "funny."

c a

k l b

Color each letter to make the word "did."

did

Find It

Cross out the word in each row that does not belong.

did	did	dine	did	did
black	black	black	black	back
every	ever	every	every	every
funny	funny	funny	fun	funny

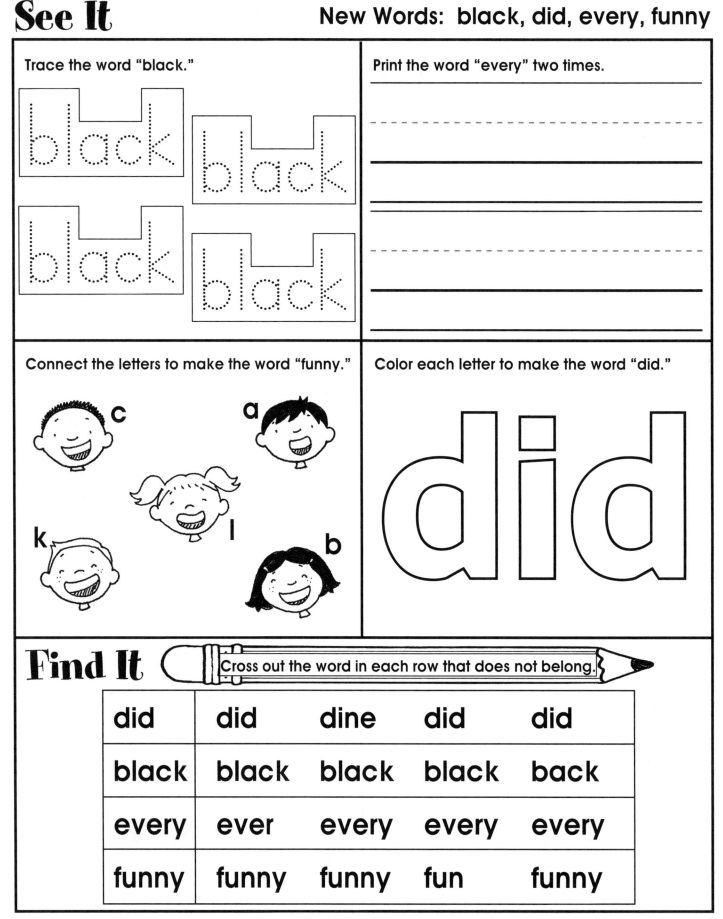

Name: _____

Directions: Cut out and paste the pictures to complete the story.

The [glue picture here] captain **did** a **funny** [glue picture here] ,

Waving his big **black** [glue picture here] .

He yelled,

"**Every** [glue picture here] must learn to [glue picture here] ."

But, they said,

"That's not in the [glue picture here] rule [glue picture here] !"

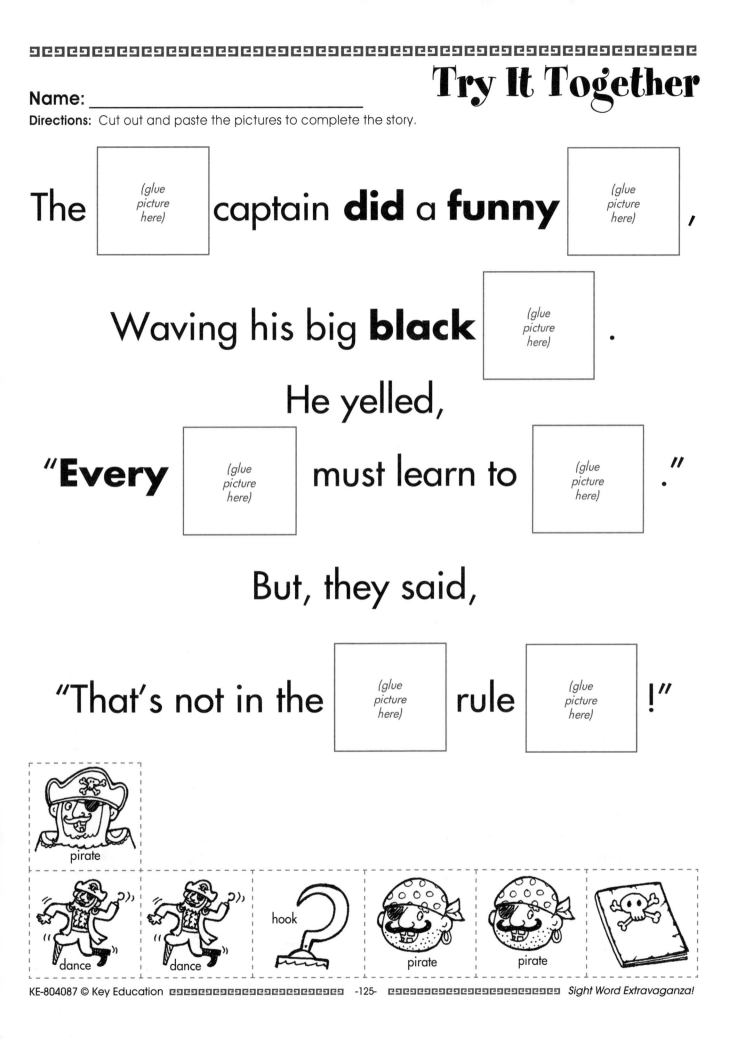

pirate

dance

dance

hook

pirate

pirate

Do It

Glitter Words

Set up a covered table with bottles of white glue, shaker bottles of glitter in different colors, and containers to catch excess glitter (one for each color). Provide each student with a pencil and four paper cards; instruct them to print one of the new sight words on each card. Next, let several students at a time take turns at the table, tracing over each printed word with white glue, sprinkling glitter on the wet glue, and then shaking the excess glitter into a container. (Return this extra glitter to the shaker bottles as needed.) After the glitter words have dried, students can use their fingers to trace over the words to "feel" how each word is spelled.

Play It

Miss Mary Mack

Teach students the clapping game Miss Mary Mack. Divide the class into pairs. Have students sit in chairs across from one another. Post the slightly modified rhyme (below) for students to see, highlighting the new sight words. Have them repeat the rhyme several times; then, teach them the motions as a group before they play the game with their partners. For an extra challenge, have students quickly stand up and sit down whenever one of the new sight words is said.

Miss Mary Mack, Mack, Mack
All dressed in <u>black</u>, <u>black</u>, <u>black</u>
With silver buttons, buttons, buttons
All down her back, back, back.
She asked her mother, mother, mother
For 50 cents, cents, cents
To see the <u>funny</u> elephant, elephant, elephant
Jump over the fence, fence, fence.
He jumped so high, high, high,
He reached the sky, sky, sky,
But he <u>did</u> come back, back, back
<u>Every</u> Fourth of July, -ly, -ly.

Do all four motions for each line of the rhyme.
1. Clap your own hands.
2. Cross your arms in front of your chest.
3. Clap your own hands together again.
4. Clap hands with your partner three times.

☆ 3 ☆

We are funny.

FOLD #1

☆ 2 ☆

We are black.

☆ 4 ☆ Every one of us.

Read It Mini-Book

> **Sight Words:**
> black, did, every, funny

FOLD #2

We did it. ☆ 1 ☆

Review It Comic Strip

See It

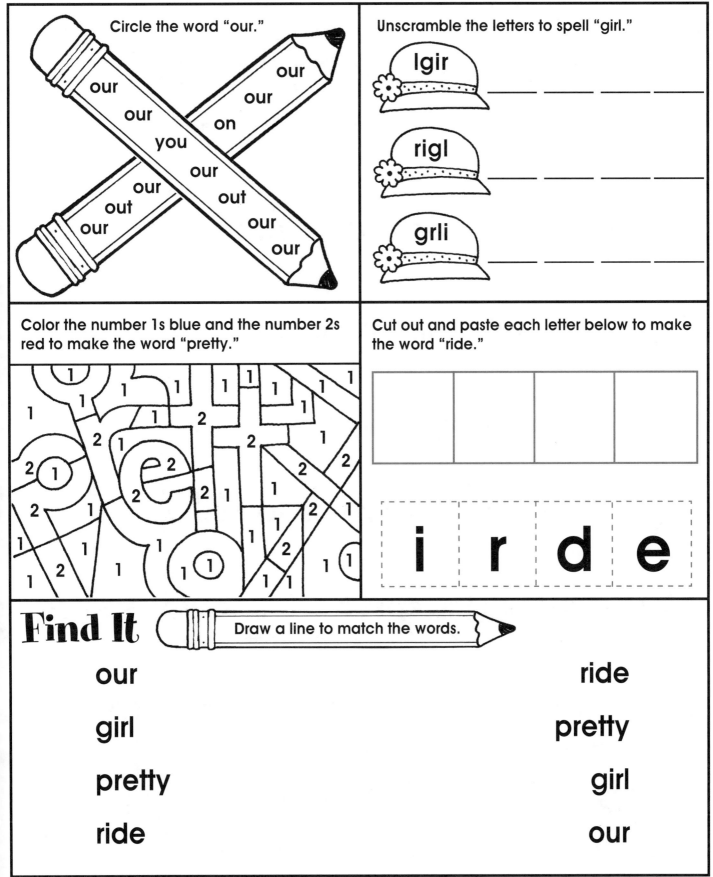

Circle the word "our."

our
our
our
our
on
you
our
our
our
out
out
our
our
our

Unscramble the letters to spell "girl."

lgir _____

rigl _____

grli _____

Color the number 1s blue and the number 2s red to make the word "pretty."

Cut out and paste each letter below to make the word "ride."

i r d e

Find It

Draw a line to match the words.

our   ride

girl   pretty

pretty   girl

ride   our

Directions: Cut out and paste the pictures to complete the story.

Try It Together

There was a **pretty** little **girl**,

Who wanted a pet to **ride**.

So, she [glue picture here] onto **our** pet [glue picture here].

Then, she fell in the mud and [glue picture here].

Our pretty little **girl**—now [glue picture here],

No longer wants to **ride**.

Our pretty little **girl** [glue picture here] away yelling,

"It's safer to [glue picture here] than to **ride**!"

jumped   cried   dirty   ran   hide

Do It

Letter Card Hunt

All around the room, clearly display alphabet letter cards that combine to spell the new sight words: *d, e, g, i, l, o, p, r, t, t, u, y*. Students will work together to find the letters to make the words. For each word, choose the same number of students as letters in the word. For example, for the word *our*, select three students to find the letters *o, u,* and *r* and assemble them to form the word for the class to see. Replace the cards and repeat the activity until each word is spelled out at least twice and each student has helped to spell at least two of the new sight words.

Play It

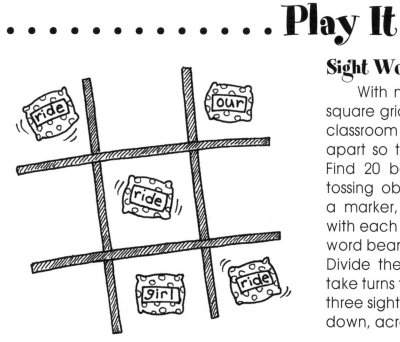

Sight Word Tic-Tac-Toe

With masking tape, create two large nine-square grids to use as tic-tac-toe boards on the classroom floor. Be sure the grids are several feet apart so that students will have room to play. Find 20 beanbags or other slightly weighted, tossing objects. Using wide masking tape and a marker, clearly label sets of five beanbags with each sight word. Place two sets of the sight word beanbags next to each tic-tac-toe board. Divide the class into pairs. Have student pairs take turns tossing their beanbags, trying to make three sight words in a row, such as *ride, ride, ride* down, across, or diagonally on the grid.

3 Our girl?

FOLD #1

2 Pretty ride.

4 Our girl!

Read It Mini-Book

Sight Words:
girl, our, pretty, ride

1 Our girl.

Review It Comic Strip

See It

Trace the word "read."

Print the word "help" two times.

Connect the letters to make the word "jump."

p

u

m

j

Color each letter to make the word "into."

into

Find It

Cross out the word in each row that does not belong.

read	read	read	read	reed
help	help	hope	help	help
into	into	tint	into	into
jump	just	jump	jump	jump

Name: _____

Directions: Cut out and paste the pictures to complete the story.

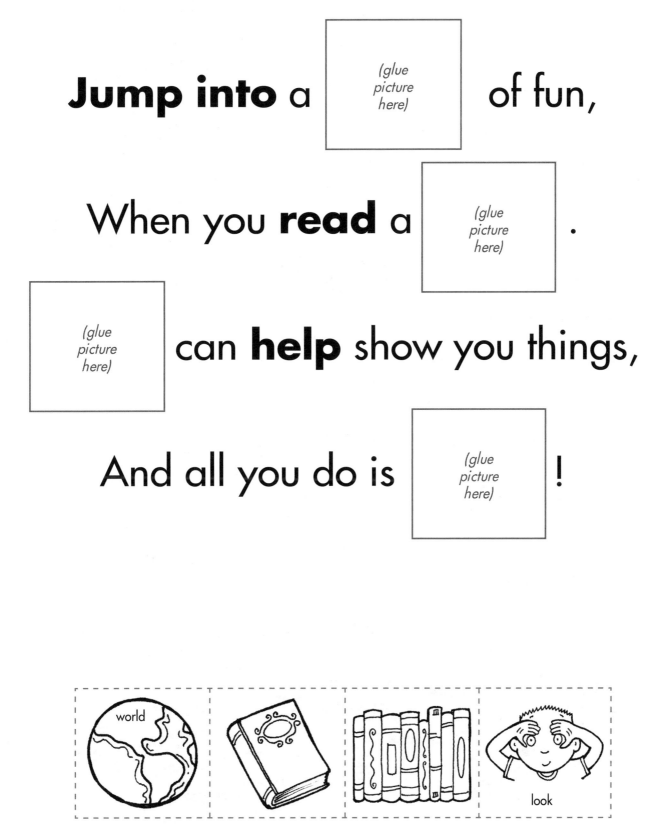

Jump into a (glue picture here) of fun,

When you **read** a (glue picture here) .

(glue picture here) can **help** show you things,

And all you do is (glue picture here) !

world

look

• • • • • • • • • • • • • Do It • • • • • • • • • • • • • •

3-D Sight Words

Collect a variety of small, colorful items used for art projects, such as buttons, paper and foam scraps, aquarium rocks, and beads. Provide each student with a large piece of drawing paper. Help students draw four writing lines horizontally (from top to bottom on the short side of the paper). Instruct students to write one of the new sight words in their biggest, neatest writing on each of the lines. Let students glue the small items on their papers, using their own writing as a guide, to make three-dimensional words.

• • • • • • • • • • • • • Play It • • • • • • • • • • • • • •

Read Sentence Strips

On paper sentence strips, one for each student, write several simple sentences that contain the new sight words. On the back of each strip, write a student's name. Place the sentence strips all over the room and then allow students to find their own strips. Have students take turns to read their sentences to the class and identify the new sight words. After students have shared their sentences, instruct them to write all four of the new sight words on the backs of the strips. See the following sample sight word sentences:

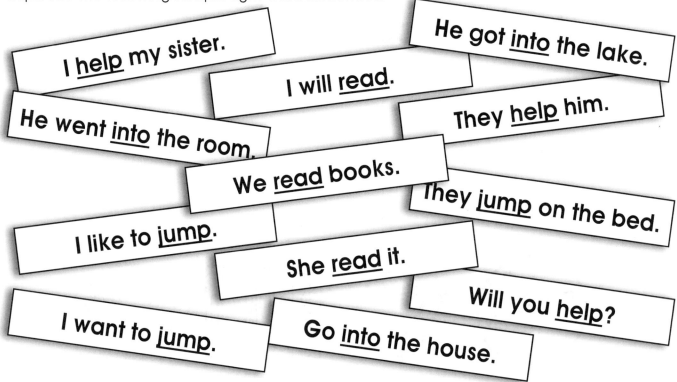

Help me jump into the water? ★3

Help me read? ★2

FOLD #1

Read It Mini-Book

Sight Words:
help, into, jump, read

★4 Help me hug?

FOLD #2

Help me? ★1

Review It Comic Strip

New Words: four, take, two, walk

Circle the word "two."

Unscramble the letters to spell "take."

aetk ___ ___ ___ ___

teka ___ ___ ___ ___

aket ___ ___ ___ ___

Color the number 1s blue and the number 2s red to make the word "walk."

Cut out and paste each letter below to make the word "four."

o r u f

Find It

Draw a line to match the words.

take   walk

two   four

walk   two

four   take

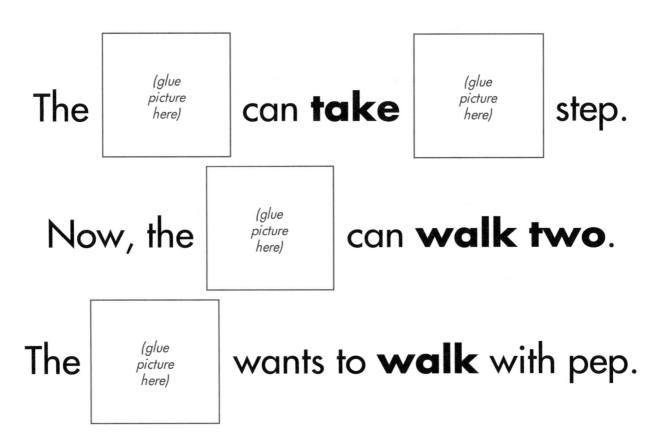

Name: _____

Try It Together

Directions: Cut out and paste the pictures to complete the story.

The [(glue picture here)] can **take** [(glue picture here)] step.

Now, the [(glue picture here)] can **walk two**.

The [(glue picture here)] wants to **walk** with pep.

But, with **four** steps,

he [(glue picture here)] "boo-hoo!"

• • • • • • • • • • • • • • • • Do It • • • • • • • • • • • • • • • • •

Key Chain Words

Cut 2" x 6" (5 cm x 15.24 cm) strips from card stock in four different colors. Punch a single hole, centered approximately 1" (2.54 cm) from the bottom of each strip. Give each student four strips in different colors and a marker. Instruct students to neatly write one of the new sight words on each strip.

Select easy reader books that contain each of the new sight words to share with the class. When a new sight word is mentioned, have students hold up their word strips labeled with the appropriate word.

Extend the activity over the next several days by giving students more of the colorful card stock strips so that they can write additional sight words they have learned. Once they have written all of their sight words, tie a loop of yarn or insert a binder ring through the holes to secure the word strips. Now, each student will have an individual, easy-to-find reference of must-know words.

• • • • • • • • • • • • • • Play It • • • • • • • • • • • • • •

Sight Word Simon Says

Play Simon Says as a class. Remind students that they must do what Simon tells them to do, as long as the command begins with "Simon says." Have half of the class be an active audience and the other half be players. Instruct the audience that whenever they hear a new sight word in one of Simon's commands, they should hold up their corresponding paper strips from the above "Do It" activity. (Alternatively, distribute word cards for students to display; see pages 154–159.) Have the audience and players switch roles after every four commands. Start the game, making sure that each of your instructions uses one of the new sight words. For example:

"Simon says <u>walk</u> in place."
"Simon says pat your head <u>two</u> times."
"Simon says <u>take</u> a baby step backward."
"Simon says hop <u>four</u> times."

Two?

Walk.

FOLD #1

Read It Mini-Book

Sight Words:
four, take, two, walk

Four.

Take him.

Review It Comic Strip

Trace the word "work."

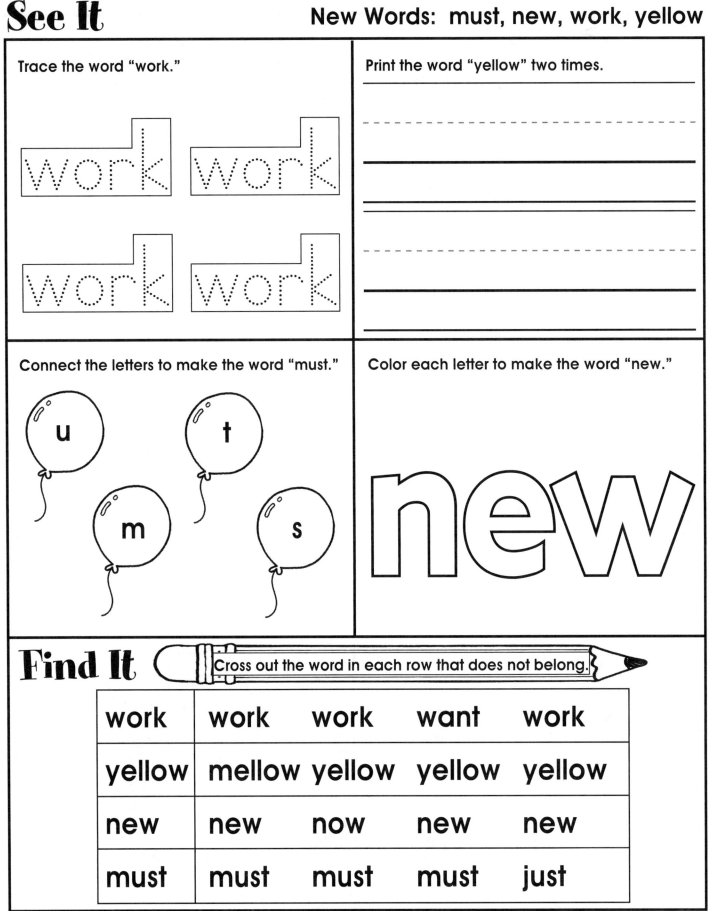

work   work

work   work

Print the word "yellow" two times.

Connect the letters to make the word "must."

u   t

m   s

Color each letter to make the word "new."

new

Find It

Cross out the word in each row that does not belong.

work	work	work	want	work
yellow	mellow	yellow	yellow	yellow
new	new	now	new	new
must	must	must	must	just

Name: _____

Directions: Cut out and paste the pictures to complete the story.

Off to **work**, I **must** go.

My **new** job will be great.

I get to _(glue picture here)_ and honk a _(glue picture here)_

And be on _(glue picture here)_ — not late!

Kids need me to get to _(glue picture here)_ .

My **new** job is a **must**.

What I _(glue picture here)_ is big and **yellow**.

My **work** is driving a _(glue picture here)_ _(glue picture here)_ .

time

school

school

drive

drive

• • • • • • • • • • • • • • • Do It • • • • • • • • • • • • • • •

Write Words with Shaving Cream

Provide each student with an aluminum pie pan and a few paper towels. Squirt a large mound of shaving cream (or whipped cream if you prefer, but students tend to eat it) in each student's pan. Call out each new sight word. As you do, instruct students to use their index fingers to write the word in the shaving cream. After each word, students can simply use their hands to gently "erase" the word and be ready for the next one. During and after the activity, students can wipe their hands with the paper towels. Your classroom will smell fresh and clean, and your students will have had some memorable, tactile practice to reinforce the new sight words.

• • • • • • • • • • • • • • Play It • • • • • • • • • • • • • •

Silly Rhyming Words

Read a few of the many funny, rhyming books by Dr. Seuss, such as *The Foot Book, Fox in Socks, Hop on Pop,* or *There's a Wocket in My Pocket!* Point out the silly and, in some cases, made-up rhymes. List the new sight words on the board or on chart paper. Have students brainstorm a list of "real" rhyming words and some fun, "pretend" rhyming words. Guide the class to make up several silly rhyming sentences using the four new sight words and the brainstormed rhyming words. Try to turn the sentences into a poem or short story for an original class creation. Post the final draft on a bulletin board with the new sight words highlighted.

<u>Real</u>
work: clerk, jerk, lurk
yellow: cello, mellow, hello, bellow
new: boo, you, glue, blew, true
must: dust, gust, rust, trust

<u>Pretend</u>
work: nerk, slirk, plurk
yellow: lellow, drellow, polyello
new: toodle-oo, plue
must: klust, vrust, nust

Silly Rhyming Story Example:

When the clerk drove to <u>work</u>, her car went jerk, and she yelled, "Urk!"
"Hello! Do not bellow! Be mellow," said the <u>yellow</u> fellow eating jello under the umbrellow."
"But, my car is <u>new</u>; that's the clue for why I'm blue. Oh, boo-hoo!"
"True? I can help you. Toodle-oo!"
"I <u>must</u> trust that the yellow fellow is not a klust."
"Oh, look—it was just dust and rust!"

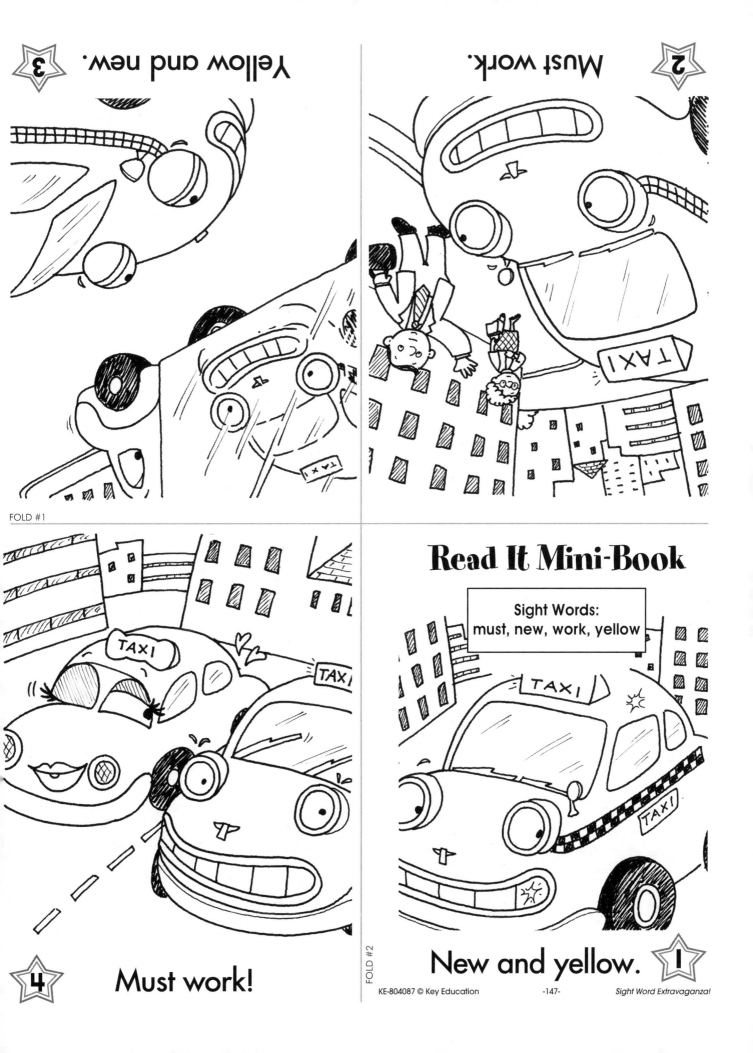

3 Yellow and new.

2 Must work.

FOLD #1

Read It Mini-Book

Sight Words:
must, new, work, yellow

4 Must work!

FOLD #2

New and yellow. **1**

Review It Comic Strip

See It

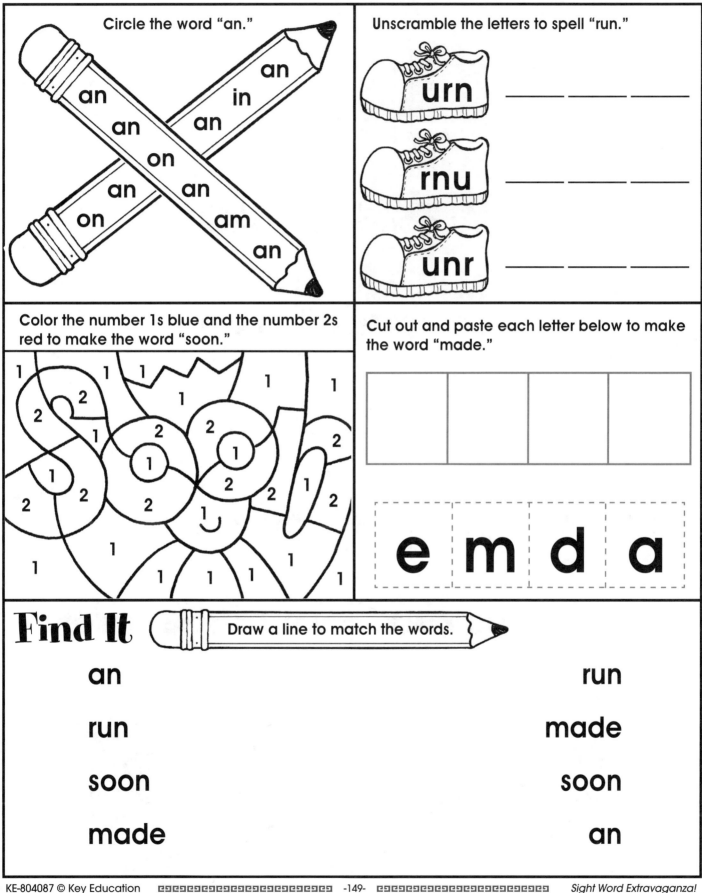

Circle the word "an."

Unscramble the letters to spell "run."

urn _ _ _

rnu _ _ _

unr _ _ _

Color the number 1s blue and the number 2s red to make the word "soon."

Cut out and paste each letter below to make the word "made."

e m d a

Find It

Draw a line to match the words.

an	run
run	made
soon	soon
made	an

Name: _____

Directions: Cut out and paste the pictures to complete the story.

(glue picture here) am **an** (glue picture here)

And a good rollerskater.

I am **made** to **run**.

It is so much fun!

Can you (glue picture here) over **soon** to (glue picture here) ?

And, we can **run** — we **made** a date.

• • • • • • • • • • • • • Do It • • • • • • • • • • • • •

Sight Word Hats

Prepare word cards, at least one for each student, by writing the new sight words separately on 3" x 5" index cards. (Alternatively, enlarge and copy the new word cards provided on pages 154–159.) Provide each student with a section of newspaper and demonstrate for students how to make a paper hat.

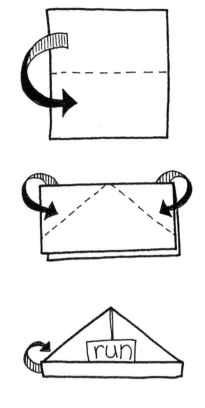

1. First, fold the paper in half horizontally from top to bottom, bringing together the short sides of the paper.

2. Bring the folded corners down to the center, leaving a few inches of paper at the bottom.

3. Fold up the paper at the bottom on each side to create a brim around the hat. Tuck in and tape the corner edges to secure them.

Have students put on their hats. Then, divide the class into pairs. Pass out a word card to each student facedown. Without looking at their cards, have students carefully place the cards in the brims of their hats so that the words face out. Next, each student in the pair will use clues to describe the word card seen in the partner's hat, such as it rhymes with moon or it begins with the letter *m*. After all students have correctly guessed the words on their cards, collect the cards and pass them out again facedown. Continue to play for several rounds.

• • • • • • • • • • • • Play It. • • • • • • • • • • • • •

Fill In the Silly Sentence

Write a variety of super-silly, funny, and gross but kid-friendly sentences that could contain the new sight words. For example: He kissed ____ anteater. (*an*) Then, write each new sight word on a different color of large self-stick notes. As you read each sentence aloud, display it on chart paper. Finally, invite a student to guess the correct word by placing the self-stick note in the sentence on the chart paper. See the following sample sentences:

> He has ____ alien in his lunchbox. (<u>an</u>)
> I like to ____ in baby booties. (<u>run</u>)
> My teacher plans to lay an egg ____ . (<u>soon</u>)
> They ____ a chocolate ant and bologna sandwich. (<u>made</u>)

Soon.

FOLD #1

Soon?

Read It Mini-Book

Sight Words:
an, made, run, soon

FOLD #2

I made an airplane. **1**

     Sight Word Extravaganza!

Review It Comic Strip

and	ate	black	but	come
an	at	big	brown	can
am	ask	be	boy	came
all	are	away	blue	by

down	for	get	good	he
do	find	funny	go	have
did	every	from	give	has
could	eat	four	girl	had

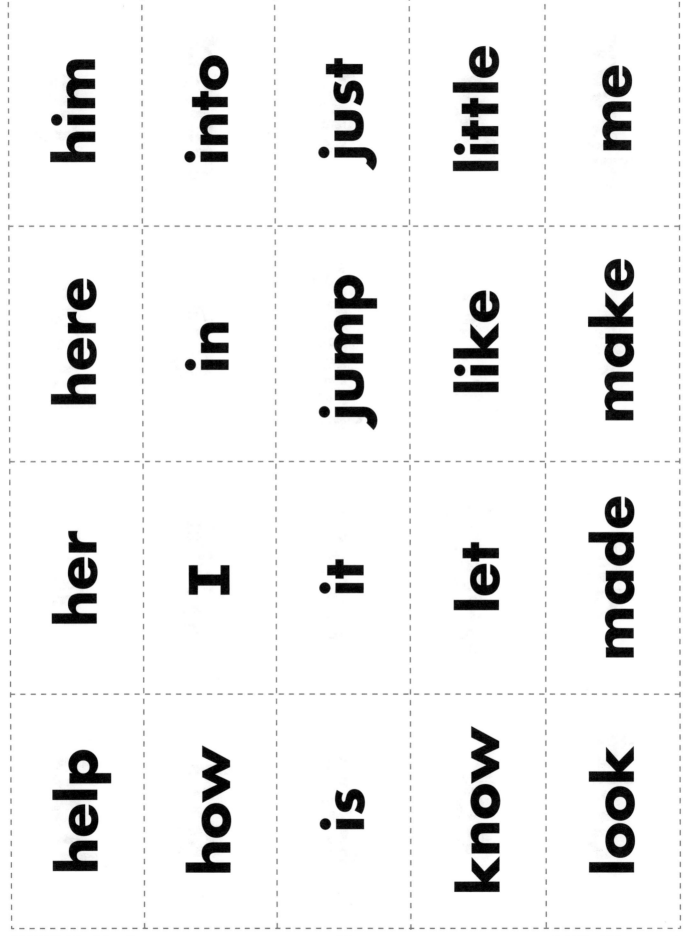

him	into	just	little	me
here	in	jump	like	make
her	I	it	let	made
help	how	is	know	look

no	on	over	put	ride
new	of	out	pretty	red
my	now	our	please	read
must	not	one	play	ran

say	saw	said	run
some	so	she	see
thank	take	stop	soon
then	them	the	that
this	think	they	there

under	was	when	with	you
two	want	what	will	yes
to	walk	went	who	yellow
three	up	we	where	work

Correlations to the Standards

This book supports the NCTE/IRA Standards for the English Language Arts and the recommended teaching practices outlined in the NAEYC/IRA position statement Learning to Read and Write: Developmentally Appropriate Practices for Young Children.

NCTE/IRA Standards for the English Language Arts

Each activity in this book supports one or more of the following standards:

1. **Students read many different types of print and nonprint texts for a variety of purposes.** Students read individual sight words, along with brief illustrated stories, comic strips, and rebus stories while doing the activities in *Sight Word Extravaganza*.

2. **Students read literature from various time periods, cultures, and genres in order to form an understanding of humanity.** Several of the units in *Sight Word Extravaganza* include activities in which teachers read literature to students.

3. **Students use a variety of strategies to build meaning while reading.** The activities in this book promote letter recognition and sight word recognition, essential skills in learning to read.

4. **Students communicate in spoken, written, and visual form, for a variety of purposes and a variety of audiences.** In this book, students communicate in spoken form by saying sight words in activities and participating in class discussions. They write sight words, and they communicate visually by drawing pictures, circling, cutting and pasting, coloring, and matching in various activities.

NAEYC/IRA Position Statement Learning to Read and Write: Developmentally Appropriate Practices for Young Children

Each activity in this book supports one or more of the following recommended teaching practices for Preschool students:

1. **Adults create positive relationships with children by talking with them, modeling reading and writing, and building children's interest in reading and writing.** The class discussions, story read-alouds, and engaging activities in *Sight Word Extravaganza* support this standard.

2. **Teachers read to children daily, both as individuals and in small groups. They select high-quality, culturally diverse reading materials.** Teachers read rebus stories, picture books, mini books, and comic strips with students throughout *Sight Word Extravaganza*.

3. **Teachers provide opportunities for children to discuss what has been read to them, focusing on both language structure and content.** *Sight Word Extravaganza* include discussions after read-alouds.

4. **Teachers promote the development of phonemic awareness through appropriate songs, finger plays, games, poems, and stories.** Many of the "Try It Together" rebus stories in *Sight Word Extravaganza* support the development of phonemic awareness through rhyme.

5. **Teachers provide opportunities for children to participate in literacy play, incorporating both reading and writing.** *Sight Word Extravaganza* includes many games and activities that incorporate reading.

6. **Teachers provide experiences and materials that help children expand their vocabularies.** *Sight Word Extravaganza* presents 120 essential sight words to students, making it a great way to expand students' vocabularies.

Each activity in this book supports one or more of the following recommended teaching practices for Kindergarten and Primary students:

1. **Teachers read to children daily and provide opportunities for students to independently read both fiction and nonfiction texts.** Teachers read picture books to students for several activities in *Sight Word Extravaganza*, and students read rebus stories, mini-books, and comic strips while doing the activities in it.

2. **Teachers provide opportunities for students to write many different kinds of texts for different purposes.** Students learn to write a variety of sight words through the activities in this book.

3. **Teachers provide opportunities for children to work in small groups.** *Sight Word Extravaganza* includes many small group activities.

4. **Teachers provide challenging instruction that expands children's knowledge of their world and expands vocabulary.** *Sight Word Extravaganza* presents 120 essential sight words to students, making it a great way to expand students' vocabularies.

5. **Teachers adapt teaching strategies based on the individual needs of a child.** *Sight Word Extravaganza* includes visual, auditory, tactile, and kinesthetic activities, so it supports a wide variety of student learning styles.